Y0-ABI-471

FILMMAKERS SERIES

edited by
ANTHONY SLIDE

1. *James Whale,* by James Curtis. 1982
2. *Cinema Stylists,* by John Belton. 1983
3. *Harry Langdon,* by William Schelly. 1982
4. *William A. Wellman,* by Frank Thompson. 1983
5. *Stanley Donen,* by Joseph Casper. 1983
6. *Brian De Palma,* by Michael Bliss. 1983
7. *J. Stuart Blackton,* by Marian Blackton Trimble. 1985
8. *Martin Scorsese and Michael Cimino,* by Michael Bliss. 1985
9. *Franklin J. Schaffner,* by Erwin Kim. 1985
10. *D.W. Griffith at Biograph,* by Cooper C. Graham, et al. 1985
11. *Some Day We'll Laugh: An Autobiography,* by Esther Ralston. 1985
12. *The Memoirs of Alice Guy Blaché,* trans. by Roberta and Simone Blaché. 1986
13. *Leni Riefenstahl and Olympia,* by Cooper C. Graham. 1986
14. *Robert Florey,* by Brian Taves. 1986
15. *Henry King's America,* by Walter Coppedge. 1986
16. *Aldous Huxley,* by Virginia M. Clark. 1987
17. *Five Cinematographers,* by Scott Eyman. 1987

In Preparation

Al Christie, by Sam Gill
Martin and Osa Johnson, by Pascal J. and Eleanor M. Imperato

Henry King's America

by

Walter Coppedge

Filmmakers, No. 15

**The Scarecrow Press, Inc.
Metuchen, N.J., & London
1986**

Library of Congress Cataloging-in-Publication Data

Coppedge, Walter, 1930-
Henry King's America.

(Filmmakers series ; no. 15)
Filmography: p.
Bibliography: p.
1. King, Henry, 1886-1982. 2. Moving-picture producers and directors--United States--Biography. I. Title. II. Series.
PN1998.A3K553 1986 791.43'0233'0924 86-22066
ISBN 0-8108-1957-0

Manufactured in the United States of American

For David Shepard
whose inspiration and guidance
made this work possible

TABLE OF CONTENTS

EDITOR'S FOREWORD

Because Henry King's career as a director was so long--lasting from 1915 through 1962--and because the type and subject of the films on which he worked was so varied, it might be argued that it would be hard to uncover any basic theme or outlook to his work. As Walter Coppedge proves here, such is not the case. A group of King's films, covering a thirty year period, offer a highly personal view of American life and society. They prove the director to be, as Gregory Peck writes in his foreword, "very American in character, old-fashioned in his ideals and in his code."

Walter Coppedge, who is a professor of English at Virginia Commonwealth University in Richmond, provides a detailed study of five features: Tol'able David (1921), Stella Dallas (1925), State Fair (1933), Jesse James (1939), and The Gunfighter (1950). Additionally, Professor Coppedge offers a useful overview of Henry King's entire career, along with a detailed chronology of his life and his films. It might, perhaps, be argued that as this is the first book on Henry King, it should be more general in scope. I would contend that Henry King's career was so varied and that King was such an original director that his career demands a series of volumes such as this, each focusing on a particular aspect of the director, who was an integral part of the film industry for more than forty-five years and who proved that commercialism did not necessarily demand a rejection of artistry.

Anthony Slide
June 1986

FOREWORD
By Gregory Peck

I had been around Twentieth-Century Fox about five years by the time I first met Henry. Darryl [F. Zanuck], who was close to Henry, was actively running the studio then and was in on everything, every script, chapter and verse. Darryl called to ask if he might send me the script of *Twelve O'Clock High*. I called back in a day or two and said, "You've got me if you want me."

I remember first meeting with Henry in the corner office on the second floor of Fox. He had a tremendous enthusiasm and relish for the project as he discussed it, telling and re-telling the story in all its aspects, and talking about my character. And the thoroughness with which he had gone into it! He had already scouted locations. As he talked to me about casting, I got the sense of a man who was relishing his work with a kind of wonderful, boyish enthusiasm--a man with vast experience and know-how.

It was very appealing to me; I liked him from the beginning. We always got along in a kind of father and son relationship. But in another way knowing Henry was like having an older brother. And in yet another way, our relationship was just one of two close friends.

I think we were cut from the same cloth, not merely as fellow actors, but more as middle Americans. He was from Virginia. I was from California. But we seemed to share a lot of easy understanding without the need for detailed discussion. The values and the standards we held up for ourselves were in many ways similar, in spite of a 30-year age difference.

He directed me in *Twelve O'Clock High*, *The Gunfighter*, *David and Bathsheba*, *The Snows of Kilimanjaro*, *The Bravados*, and *Beloved Infidel*, and these pictures reflect honor, integrity, being true to your word, living up to your commitments. They say: don't lie; don't cheat; don't use anybody; be open-hearted and generous; do your duty; be a man--what some people would now think are old-fashioned virtues. We never articulated those precepts; we never said, "Now we're going to reflect these values." Without much analysis, we just talked about the story and the characters.

Because he was a really fine producer and a studio head of the old school, Darryl saw that rapport between us. That must be why he kept putting us together.

When we talked over a script, it was story and character that interested us, not the psychoanalysis of the character or the search for inner motives--just clarifying the fit of each scene into the sequence of events, what went before and what was to follow. In the same way, we discussed character behavior. Our talks were directed to the practical and pragmatic, and not to the dissection of the character's "inner being." That was left to me to provide from my own skills. There was a kind of line drawn, unmentioned, unarticulated. We dealt with things in a very practical way.

Henry, a talkative fellow, liked to go into great detail, but he would not do that on the set. He might talk things over extensively before a picture began, but on the set it was "get on with it." We came to the scene fully prepared.

Henry's tendency toward melodrama came from his original theatre experience. As a young man, he played in a lot of melodrama. His approach was, "If we're going to give them East Lynne, give them East Lynne. Give it to the hilt. Don't soften it or toy with it or ridicule it; give it to them and make them believe it." Henry had a rather nice, old-fashioned fondness for things that were melodramatic and theatrical, dramatic forms from which he liked to extract full value.

He liked staging. He had great experience as a stage actor, so he liked placing people and moving them about. He had a general pattern of movement worked out ahead of time, and he would say, "Now you try starting the speech sitting down there, and maybe when you get to this line, you get up and look out the window." Sometimes he would walk it through himself.

I might fall in with it or I might have a different idea, because I always enjoyed doing homework. I could not walk on the set without knowing the scene and my lines well enough to give a performance. All it needed was a knowledgeable observer to sit back and be objective, to say, "You know, I think a little bit more of this or less of that... or have you thought of this?" Henry put the polish on the performance.

That is the way we would work. Once in a while he would have an idea I did not agree with, about interpretation, movement, or business, and I would suggest a change. We would talk it over, and he would very often give me my way without any rancor or any sense of my being a meddlesome actor.

The other side of the coin is that very often he would contribute things that had never occurred to me, valuable observations, insights into character or behavior. So it was give and take, and it always worked. We felt a kinship like brothers.

Sometimes, he would play me for half a page just to show me how he thought it would go. He relished doing that; he would always have a kind of grin, an enthusiasm and playfulness on his face. He loved the work.

His approach was professional, businesslike, and playful at the same time--an approach common to fine old-timers like Raoul Walsh and William Wellman. They were thoroughly professional, but they had a sense of fun which seemed to say: "Let's tell a good story. Let's spin a yarn here."

We particularly liked doing The Gunfighter. Early on, when we started preparing the picture and I had accepted the role, both of us decided that we wanted this fellow to look and to dress in a motley collection of clothes like the people in the daguerrotypes of the early West. You see them with swallow-tail coats and hard hats and ill-fitting homespun garments. They do not look like rodeo cowboys at all, and a very large number of the men wear beards and moustaches. So Henry and I decided that I should look like one of those fellows. We pored over all the books that we could find and located several models, long, lean, tough, semi-educated, early Westerners--people who might have come out from the East or even as far away as Scotland or England. They were out there to try to make a better life. I put on a handle-bar mustache and a funny-looking, swallow-tail corduroy coat. They gave me a soup-bowl haircut, a fifteencenter--not at all romantic-looking. Then we started.

By that time, Darryl, for some reason or another, was not around, and Spyros Skouras was in Europe. After we had gone a couple of weeks, Skouras came back. It was his custom to catch up on the rushes of current productions. He let out a yowl when he saw me on the screen. He said, "What the hell is that? Who gave you that haircut? Who put a moustache on Greg Peck? He's a sex symbol. Women don't like men with moustaches. And that funny-looking haircut and that crazy-looking suit? And a black hat?" He said, "You'll ruin it. The picture won't do any business at all." He went into a rage about it, and the message came down to us on the set that Skouras was thinking about re-shooting the first two weeks.

We were very disturbed, because we liked the way that it looked on the screen. We did a little fast shuffle with the production manager, because we knew that Skouras would ask him how much it would cost to redo the first two weeks. He padded the figure. We guessed that Skouras would go for so much but not for more than that. Apparently it worked because, although he was disgusted, he did not want to spend that money to do the first two weeks over.

So, we stayed with the handlebar mustache and the funny-looking clothes. Skouras never forgot it. For twenty years, every time I saw him it was "You Black Irishman. You liar! You ruined my picture." I am half-Irish, and he would say, "Anyway, you don't even know who you are or what you are. You think the Black Irish came from the sinking of the Spanish Armada. That's bull-shit. It comes from the Greeks who were there 2,000 years ago. Where do you think you got the name Gregory anyway?"

The picture got wonderful reviews but it was not a moneymaker. It could not have been a big loser because it did not cost much--but in those days, we talked in different numbers. I doubt that they spent more than a million on it.

There was a lack of hokum in that film and a crispness in the writing. It was as truthful a version of life on the frontier as we could make.

Once the two of us flew from Florida to Los Angeles in 1949 in his Beechcraft. I was a little jumpy about being up there in a single-engine craft. Henry seemed to me like an old man then. Actually, he was a very hale 63, but to me that was old. I thought, "The man might have a heart attack up here at 12,000 feet." So I watched closely. And I watched the things on the radio, as we crossed over different towns and he talked to control. I was glued to those little levers and dials. I had on a pair of earphones and I told myself that if he suddenly became ill or had a heart attack, I might have a chance of getting myself down. (Today, 63 does not seem old to me at all.)

We had to duck the weather and fly under 12,000 feet because we had no oxygen. Those big thunderheads rolled up above, and we would go 150 miles out of the way to get around them. He was a careful, cautious flyer, business-like and thorough as he was about everything. He flew a plane most of his life, probably for 65 years--and never had an accident. After we got up I enjoyed the flight and he let me fly the plane. We were good companions.

We would come down and refuel at several spots along the way during this two-day trip. At a place called Big Spring, Texas, we spent the night. He showed a delight in talking about our motel alongside the airport. "You go there," he said, "and they make the best gin martini. They've got the biggest, juiciest green olives...." He described all this to me, and when we got there we enjoyed just the kind of evening he had me anticipating. The next day, we got up early and set off for Los Angeles.

In Henry's blue eyes there was always a sparkle. There was a kind of playful challenge, always couched in an affectionate way, and never demeaning, as if to say: "Let's see what you can do. Let's play this game together. Let's give the best we've got."

Something that has not been said yet is that he had a devastating effect on women. He was in his 60s when I first met him, but when he talked to a woman and he hit her with those blue eyes, she turned to jelly. He was charming: he was a courtier, affectionate without ever crossing the line--but it was definitely man-woman stuff. They knew that he was a man and he was aware of their femininity. That was part of the richness of his personality.

There are directors who are uneasy with women. They do not know where to place them, how to talk to them. He had a way of making them feel feminine, making them feel loved, amusing them. Henry was handy with stories to loosen them up, getting them to laugh. Then he would level those blue eyes. Even at 65, several of them said that when he looked at them they thought that he was looking right straight on through, that their knees were turning soft.

He was equally liked by men and women.

The Bravados was interesting because of Henry's change of the original script, which was a pretty straight story of man who finds his wife raped and murdered. In this outpost his tiny daughter is left psychologically damaged. He goes after the murderers and he kills them one by one. Henry's sense of morality, his Christian belief, is that revenge is wrong, that it is immoral for a man to set himself up as the judge, jury, and executioner. He would not swallow that story of pursuit and revenge. He caused it to be rewritten so that a fourth man and his wife make me--the hunter and the pursuer--their captive. Then I learn I have killed the wrong three men, that I have been on the wrong trail the whole time. I go back to the town. It was Henry's idea that we resolve the picture by having me confess to a priest. At the end Joan Collins and I come walking out of the church with my little daughter. There was a kind of a happy resolution. All that was entirely Henry's doing.

He would not direct a picture that seemed to approve of a man who went out, sought and gained revenge, and executed three men who had raped and killed his wife. This vengefulness made the role very unusual and difficult to play. I do not care for the picture much because my character is unbelievably grim and straight-faced: the protagonist has this obsession to rid the world of these rotten people. When Henry Silva told me that the dead men have not done it, my reaction to this news--and the change that takes place in my character, knowing that in my blind rage I had killed three innocent men--is, to my mind, the best scene in the picture. These victims were no good, they were thieves, but they had not killed my wife. The business in the church was very difficult to do: it was an epilogue, his "getting religion." The scene came as a surprise to me because I did not know that Henry had these strongly felt moral convictions, which seemed almost out of character.

On Beloved Infidel there were some disagreements between us. Although it was the story of Sheila Graham, I did not want to play it that way. I wanted it to be "the last episode in the life of F. Scott Fitzgerald." As such, she was incidental to the life of a great writer. She comforted him, but what is of interest about that? What interested me was her relationship with Scott Fitzgerald and his death. I kept pushing all the time to shape the story in this way. I must say that for the most part Henry resisted me. He wanted to tell Sheila Graham's story, for they had Deborah Kerr. But I kept pushing, and I got Sy Bartlett in to help rewrite what was, in truth, an awful script. Deborah and I both did it to kill off final commitments we had at Fox. I also knew that people were going to criticize me because I was not stocky, blond and blue-eyed. Practically everybody knows what Scott Fitzgerald looked like.

There was some pushing and tugging between Henry and me. It never got to the point of a shouting match, but there was tension. I was pushing one way and he was pulling another. I was pretty determined, and I got the studio to bring in a writer whom I liked. Consequently, there was work on the script during the shooting. I was determined to play an American writer who happened to be tall and dark. In my mind, it could have been Steinbeck, it could have been any American writer who had flawed genius. It was a showy part. Some of the best work I have done is in that picture, despite a patchwork script over which the studio and the star were at odds. I still think that I was right. If you have Scott Fitzgerald, you do not make him secondary to a woman like Sheila Graham. It was the last episode in the life of Scott Fitzgerald, not the rags-to-riches story of a cockney girl.

I was determined to play the living daylights out of it. I had a big drunk scene. I pushed her and slapped her around. She ran for a gun and I wrestled it away from her. Finally, the gun went off and brought me to my senses. Well, I had rehearsed that at home about 200 times. We rehearsed it on the set, and while they were setting it up I had a couple of good shots of vodka to set me on edge--because I wanted to go all out. I wanted there to be a certain wildness and an uncontrolled frustration and fury in this man. Because I decided to help myself out that way, I knew exactly what I was doing, and the alcohol did give that extra edge; but Henry smelled it on my breath, and I know he was shocked. He did not say anything to me but he said something to others. Still we got a hell of a scene out of it.

I like to think about Henry. I like to think that all that time with him was good. He helped shape my character, and he did a lot to shape my screen image, personality, and manner of performing--whatever you may call it.

I think that I learned by example, not so much by what he told me but by his being the kind of man he was and the personal code that he had. I also think him as very American in character, old-fashioned in his ideals and in his code: extremely conscientious, kind and considerate with everybody on the set, but demanding and tough when things did not go right. He had steel in him. Those times were among the best of my working life. We both looked forward to the enjoyment of going to rushes together and watching a scene come out the way we wanted. I know that we both drove home feeling fine, satisfied that we had done a good day's work. It was probably a closer relationship than I have with some of my blood relatives. There was admiration and love and respect in it, and it has not changed to this day.

Gregory Peck
Los Angeles
November 1983

Henry King
1886-1982

Chapter 1
Henry King: The Man and the Medium

King Vidor once told the English film scholar Kevin Brownlow, "I'm a pioneer. I've been in this business for years. But when I first got to Hollywood, Henry King was going strong."[1]

That was in 1915. King had already been in pictures for three years--after a chance meeting with Wilbert Melville of the Lubin Western Studios deflected him from the theatre into a career in films which would span 50 years.

When he died at the age of 96 in 1982, King was among the last of the giants, one of the last filmmakers who had significantly contributed to the medium at critical junctures of its development. He was among the earliest to experiment with fragmentation of action through editing, and among the first Americans to shoot a film in panchromatic stock, to receive possessive credit, and to develop contrapuntal sound. He was the first to make pictures overseas after World War I and to scout for locations from the air. King was among the earliest to leave his studio for American locales, to use color outdoors, and to employ the widescreen and stereophonic sound. He was the last surviving founder of the Motion Picture Academy of Arts and Sciences. Few in the history of film, after Griffith, can be said to have discovered or developed more talent. He was the most successful contract director in the history of the studio, having won by 1941 more citations for All-Time Best Sellers from the Motion Picture Almanac than any filmmaker, Chaplin excepted, who alone equalled King's five. In 1969, the last year before mega-hits became relatively routine, the International Motion Picture Almanac listed the 100 most successful pictures of all time. King's name alone appeared six times, after which, trailing in second place with four apiece, were Griffith, Lean, and Wyler, followed by John Ford with three.[2]

That these statistics may come as a surprise is an indication of the present state of King's critical fortunes. When Paul Rotha's monumental work The Film till Now appeared in 1930, King was considered in a category with Stroheim and Flaherty; King's pictures even then, Rotha concluded, did not receive the attention they deserved. Five years after the coming of sound, Dwight Macdonald, among the most acute critical intelligences in film and letters, placed King among world-class directors.[3] In the industry his value is indicated by the fact that he was chosen to make pictures for the nation's foremost producers: Ince, Goldwyn, Zanuck, and Selznick. Finally, there is Frank Capra's glowing tribute:

> Henry King, the most underpublicized filmmaker in Hollywood, belongs on anybody's "First Five" list. An inventory of his great pictures is the history of films.... Still flying his own plane in the seventies, this lean, tall, handsome, urbane, but unflamboyant model of a corporation president makes film hits so easily, so efficiently, and so calmly that he is not news in a community of blaring trumpets, crashing cymbals, and screaming egos.[4]

During his time in the industry, King was held in the royal esteem his name suggests.

While there have been retrospectives in the last ten years and a sprinkling of admiring articles, the fact is that the name Henry King, in the minds of most movie-goers, does not fuse synaptically with those indelible images that are in the memory of those who have seen his pictures. A viewer who sees these films will not forget:

*Barthelmess as David in his barrel at the swimming hole;

*Gish, luminous in her gown, as she takes her vows as the bride of Christ;

*Belle Bennett, on a rainy night, gazing longingly at the window where her daughter, radiant in bridal finery, is being married;

*James Dunn, storming the dismal poorhouse, kicking away a pail of water, and picking his mother up to carry her off;

*Janet Gaynor riding to the stars on a roller-coaster with Lew Ayres;

*Henry Fonda cavorting in a field of oats with Rochelle Hudson;

*A stricken mother (a nameless player) seen through the window of a diphtheria ward, who is watching a priest administer the last rites to her dying child;

*A chorus of Yanks singing "It's a Long Way to Tipperary" as they march off a Broadway stage through a cheering audience to the waiting ships;

*Jesse James silhouetted against the blue evening as he scrambles across the roofs of passenger coaches whose windows are golden with lamplight;

*The departing soldier turning as he descends the staircase to say to Claudette Colbert, "Stay right there, so I can always remember you this way";

*The cold Gladys Cooper as Mother Superior, envious of the grace God has given the simple Bernadette;

*The torchlight parades and the thousands massed in Baltimore for the Democratic convention of 1912 cheering the nomination of Woodrow Wilson;

*The wistful would-be flapper who one spring night watches her neighbor Charleston on the front porch to "A Cup of Coffee, Some Candy, and You";

*Orson Welles as Cesare Borgia lording it superbly in a Renaissance _palazzo_ over an opulent assembly of nobles;

*The pale hyena prowling in the night around the tent of the ailing Gregory Peck;

*Jennifer Jones running to meet William Holden on a windswept hill high above Hong Kong;

*The enchantingly glamorous beach party, festive with cocktails and music, on the Riviera of the 1920s.

For those who followed the films of Henry King, there are no doubt countless other scenes etched sharply on the tables of memory during the 45 years that King directed movies.

There is the powerful narrative sweep of such engaging minor masterpieces as _Over the Hill_ (1930) and _Remember the Day_ (1940). Even King's routine pictures in his best period (ca. 1936-1946) are filled with life: the derivative _Maryland_ (1940) betters its prototype _Kentucky_ (1938); and _A Yank in the R.A.F._ (1941) features handsome principals in a love story set in World War II London. _The Black Swan_ (1942) recounts Ben Hecht's action-packed pirate story with parodic touches in an immensely colorful Caribbean setting. Every picture King ever made offers the viewer an engrossing opening, and the spectacle-finales to such pictures as _The White Sister_ (1923), _The Winning of Barbara Worth_ (1926), and _In Old Chicago_ (1938) are vibrantly exciting. The strong pacing of _Alexander's Ragtime Band_ (1938), _Jesse James_, and _Stanley and Livingston_ (both 1939) is apparent to anyone who will simply watch the films.[5]

Those who do not watch his work carefully may find it wanting in recognizable style. King's is not the kind of creative talent that can be identified as auteurist. In the 1960s, when American directors in this country began to receive the critical attention that French theorists had paid them a decade earlier, _auteur_ was the key term in the critical vocabulary of the time. A novice critic thus possessed an instrument which allowed him to find value wherever there was a signature: thus even those with limited film experience could find Welles in ceiling shots and multiple mirrors; discover the texture in Sternberg's lattices and feathers; identify the male bonding in the comedies and Westerns of Hawks; probe the sly visual wit in Lubitsch's boudoirs and boulevardiers; observe the ironic juxtapositions of Stroheim's innocents and predators; and so on.

Upon first viewing, however, King's pictures--even his good ones--bear no distinctive cynosure, seem to show no shaping authorial presence. And for a clear reason: King never fancied himself an artist; he was a storyteller. Far from calling attention to the teller of the tale, the first duty of the director is to efface himself so that the story is not encumbered by ostentatious or attention-getting narrative mannerisms. He often recounted hearing Irving S. Cobb, the popular American humorist of the 1920s and 30s, tell a story at a luncheon which was side-splittingly funny; one month later he heard the same story, and it wasn't funny at all.[6] As King recognized, the definition of style is "the way you tell a story."[7] What is distinctive in King's style is a simplicity of transmission, the meditative contemplation of humanity from the middle distance, the creation of a controlling mood in harmony with the psychology of a scene, the unobtrusive yet carefully planned symmetry of a visual composition, and the appropriate integration (usually subordinal) of aural elements. The fact that these qualities are not conspicuous is, in effect, King's art as a filmmaker. As King once observed, "When direction shows, it's bad."[8]

At the same time, King would have been the first to call motion pictures a collaborative endeavor. "No one person ever made a motion picture," he would say, "yet everyone makes the picture."[9] By "everyone" King meant producers, writers, cinematographers, editors, actors, musicians, and scores of ancillary technicians. Some of these he came to depend upon year after year: Zanuck was his chief and greatly admired producer; scenarists he repeatedly worked with included Jules Furthman, Frances Marion, Sonya Levien, Lamar Trotti, Sy Bartlett, and Casey Robinson. For 20 years Robert Webb was an able and devoed assistant director; for 30 years Barbara McLean cut his pictures (she usually had two takes to choose from, as King aimed to print the first take);[10] and from 1942 on Leon Shamroy was his favorite cameraman (he worked with King on 14 pictures). These talented people he involved so closely in his work that after a few years McLean could read his thoughts and Shamroy, who carefully watched King rehearse, could anticipate his lighting and set-ups. That they collaborated with him in the fashioning of a film does not diminish the art and skill of the director, whose work is to coordinate their endeavors in the service of the story--a story which has to pass through the mind of a controlling intelligence.

All of King's good pictures are strongly unified thematically. They would have to be if King's repeated dictum about telling a story clearly has any relation to his practice. As King explained to a journalist, "A story conveys a thought and the moment you deviate from it you are lost. We [filmmakers] can still tell a good story better than any other medium."[11] Thus _Tol'able David_ (1921) is about a boy's passage from wishful adolescence into responsible manhood; _State Fair_ (1932) about a family's journey and the quest of each of them--father, mother, son, daughter--for the appropriate recognition or experience; _Jesse James_ (1939) about Robin Hood, American-style in a Depression-emergent context; Stanley and Livingston (1939) about life transformed through the example of inspired service; Remember the Day (1940) about the love of a fourth-grader for his teacher in the America of the early teens; Twelve O'Clock High (1949) about the awful burden of responsibility under intolerable pressures; The Gunfighter (1950) about a weary winner aware of the vanity of his title, but who cannot retire from the contest.

Part of King's signal success as a director was his ability to work sensitively and harmoniously with those whose craft he had himself practiced. Actors rarely continue to work with directors who treat them unfeelingly. The record is that King made seven pictures with H. B. Warner, eleven with William Russell, five with Richard Barthelmess, three with Pauline Frederick, three with Ronald Colman, four with Susan Hayward, eleven with Tyrone Power, and six with Gregory Peck.

The list of names he introduced and developed in the medium is impressively long. Some became stars of the first magnitude; some rose and flared with meteoric intensity. Not many people will remember the great acclaim which greeted King's first picture for Ince, the lost 23 1/2 Hours Leave (1919) and which made a star of Douglas Maclean. Still fewer will recall the first popular child star, Baby Marie Osborne, who faded after she was six. But those who know films of the 1920s will remember the menacing Ernest Torrence, a Scottish operatic baritone whose notable motion picture career King launched. When a stiff and uncertain English stage actor thought he could have no future in American pictures, King combed back his hair, pencilled a moustache, and gave Ronald Colman the confidence which enabled him to become one of the screen's most graceful and civilized presences. With Goldwyn he introduced to American films the radiant ingenue Lois Moran. He discovered a long and lean Montana cowboy and gave Gary Cooper his first screen appearance. He taught Don Ameche, a camera-shy radio personality, how to become an unselfconscious actor. Once he found a bit player about to be dropped from production, and overnight he convinced Zanuck to star Tyrone Power in the studio's biggest picture that year. King tested an English tourist for the role of an aristocratic scoundrel and so started George Sanders on his career in this country as one of the screen's most interesting personalities. He salvaged Alice Faye, wounded by directorial insensitivity, as she was about to pack her bags and flee to New York. He took an ingenue who had done a Western and a Dick Tracy serial and bestowed stardom on Jennifer Jones. He tested the winner of a beauty contest from Cleveland and started Jean Peters on her way to fame and fortune. He launched Ava Gardner as a serious dramatic actress and extracted from Errol Flynn his finest screen performance.

King can be credited with saving Jean Hersholt's faltering career three times until at last he found a role in The Country Doctor (1936), which he would then play throughout his life. Fox's biggest male star in the 1930s was sliding until King let Will Rogers play himself in State Fair. Belle Bennett came to the greatest role of her career with King, and Mae Marsh once again found her chance for stardom in the talkies under King's direction. Others who benefited by his sure guidance were Louise Dresser, Alice Brady, and Margaret Hamilton. The dramatic iconography in twentieth-century pictures (not to say of Twentieth-Century Fox) would surely have been different had there been no Henry King.

King's understanding of acting was indeed one of his directorial strengths. "Acting," said King, "is just human nature." When the actors and the director have a complete understanding of what they're doing, good acting happens naturally.[12] Directing is simplicity itself, he pointed out. In a scene the director must get down to the heart of the subject, what it is about: both to the feelings of the characters and to those who are interpreting the parts. When James Stewart reflected on King's direction of him, he responded that King "was primarily interested in getting the story on the screen, in telling the story as visually as possible.... As an actor I found him easy to work with."[13] In telling that story, King wrote Scott Eyman that the story has to be told as the director sees it--therefore he must give actors his impression of the characters as well as of the story. This gives the actor something definite to work on and enables him to show his creative ability more than if he read the story and gave his own interpretation.[14] He praised Ava Gardner and Jennifer Jones for their intuitive understanding (understanding, however, that the director has first to communicate) so that they get a scene right the first time. There were not enough outtakes from Bernadette to make a trailer.[15]

King found it necessary to vary his techniques according to the actors he was working with. Alice Faye had been so intimidated by a bullying director that she could not remember a line. King would cut when she forgot, praise her, order prints (to Zanuck's consternation: he was astonished at the bits and pieces on the rushes that first day), thus building her confidence until she was strong enough to sail through her first starring role in In Old Chicago.[16] According to studio publicist Harry Brand, when an actor happened to blow a line, King's strategy would be to blame himself or some mechanical setup.[17] Faye, who eventually became the country's top female star at the box office, credited King with giving her career its greatest boost.[18] Similarly, Mae Marsh was so frightened of the microphone that she could not get through a scene--"I don't know a bee from a bull's foot about saying anything," she complained. When filming Over the Hill,

King fed her the lines and told her to concentrate on what she was saying, not how she was saying it.[19]

With Errol Flynn, King recollected that acting did not come easily; his tendency was to rush through a scene to get it over with... "but we would talk for hours about Mike's state of mind [in The Sun Also Rises]. I told him not to worry about not projecting the emotions of the scene because once he had thought his interpretation through, the emotions would take care of themselves; and that is what happened. We did his long speech on the first take."[20]

Tyrone Power's acting problem was unusual. If he tried too hard, he would dissipate the force of a scene: he came across as weak. "When Ty was quiet, he could show more strength than if he rose up and tried to shout."[21]

The evidence is that a wide variety of actors testify that King was an extremely good director to work with. Janet Gaynor, who made four films with him, remembered him as "an excellent director, unlike some who waste their time planning on the set. King was business-like and knew exactly what he wanted."[22] Jean Peters remembers that if she survived in her first part (the taxing role of the peasant girl in Captain from Castile) it was because of King.[23] Ralph Bellamy remembered especially that he "treated actors with great respect."[24] Gary Merrill acknowledged that King was "considerate" and "let the actors pretty much alone, although giving us leeway on a good script" (Twelve O'Clock High, whose final script revision King oversaw). Eddie Albert remembered that King was easy to work with, that he showed no weakness, and that sometimes he did give actors leeway (The Sun Also Rises).[25]

King was keenly aware that an actor has to have emotions if he is going to be able to use them. The actor must therefore necessarily possess a sensitivity which needs to be protected and channeled: "He has to have feelings... you get them stirred up in the wrong way and in that state of confusion an actor doesn't know what to do."[26] Perhaps his great gift was to make actors feel that his ideas were originally their ideas. Joseph Hergesheimer once visited him during a rehearsal: "You know," he reflected, "I feel I have learned a great deal about directing from watching. What you do is get an idea and roll it up, and then you catch the actor with his mouth open, and you toss it in there, and it comes out as his own idea."[27] "I don't believe you can just tell a person what to do," King said. Every situation in the script King tested to determine its playability. "I walk through the scene myself, trying not to have the actor see me.... If I can't walk through it, I don't ask anyone else to."[28] This awareness of the problems of the actor extended even to bit players. A person who has half a page of dialogue needs to be inspired, needs to have the same feeling for the script as one who has worked for weeks on it, needs to think it through for himself. "When he fits, he belongs to the cast."[29]

King's contribution to the actor's art was not in just the communication of shared understanding and in the sympathetic handling of ego. The director must guide actors in the rhythm of a scene and assist them in meeting problems and in building characterization. Spencer Tracy was very discouraged about delivering a line so famous that it had become a cliché. How could he say, "Dr. Livingston, I presume?" All he could think of was a joke about a white man who wanders into a bar in Harlem. The bar is filled with blacks, but at the end of the room he espies another white man sitting alone over his drink. He walks up to him and says, "Dr. Livingston, I presume?" Thinking of that line, Tracy knew they'd be laughed out of the theatre; the line couldn't be said. King walked over to him and paused. "The man has swamp fever. He can hardly walk. He comes into the clearing. "Dr." -pant- "Livingston" -pant- "I presume?" Tracy grinned in reply: "I could kill you. You've played the scene for me, and I didn't have sense enough to think about it."[30]

In Remember the Day, John Payne was faced with the problem of communicating his high spirits during a honeymoon scene. King recalls suggesting, "John, if it were me, I would bounce over and hit the bed. He did so, the bed broke, and he and his bride hit the floor. Claudette Colbert was screaming with laughter. I made that the finish of the sequence. It was just a perfect climax."[31]

On the same picture, the writer Allen Scott came up to King and told him there was a problem: what happens to the husband after he gets on the train to go to war? Since the picture is a love story between a boy and his teacher, it was clear that the character played by Payne would have to be removed, would have to be killed. When King told Colbert and her two women colleagues in the picture that the husband would be killed in Europe, the three started crying. King immediately objected: "Shut up! We're not doing that kind of scene. You must be able to control your emotions. With tears from you, there's none in the audience." King remembered that when Colbert did the scene, it was one of the most emotional he had ever seen--and it was as "cold-blooded" as it was possible to be. That sort of disciplined control of the emotions King considered essential for good acting. An actor who is emotionally aloof from his role will turn in the best performance, King once told a reporter. To identify completely with the characterization is the notion of the amateur, indeed almost of the ham. King remembered that when he was directing Gish and Colman in The White Sister, the crew would be ready to weep, but that at the last shot--so superbly unemotional were they as players--they would walk away casually.[32]

King directing apprehensive Spencer Tracy in Stanley and Livingston (1939).

Lillian Gish and Ronald Colman in The White Sister (1923).

Henry also recalled Lionel Barrymore in Carolina (1934). Barrymore was Barrymore until the moment he walked onto the set; then he assumed the character of the crusty old patriarch. He would look at Henrietta Crosman, playing his sister-in-law, and mutter loudly enough for her to hear, "Oh, is that old bitch out here again this morning?" When he would leave the set, he would leave the part. King remembered that working with him was a great pleasure.[33]

Samuel Goldwyn once observed that if a director does not lose more than five or ten percent of a script, he's a good director. "Some directors can add five to ten percent; those are the great ones."[34] King frequently contributed that margin to help actors flesh out their roles. King remembered telling Ernest Torrence that Luke Hatburn in Tol'able David picks up a stone to strike a cat, not out of malice, but from a depraved and ignorant curiosity--to see the guts spill.[35] On another occasion he remembered seeing on the Piazza di Spagna a black musician who had been left behind by a touring orchestra. As the man was extremely hungry, he solicited passersby to help, but he was constantly rebuffed because he didn't speak Italian. When King's companion replied to him in English, he embraced him in excitement and fainted. King incorporated this response in Ketti Gallian's portrayal of a French woman in Panama who at last finds someone who speaks her language (Marie Galante, 1934).[36] To suggest a European ambience in a hotel scene in The Woman Disputed, King remembered seeing a man kiss the hand of a woman waiting in the lobby. When her escort arrives, he takes out his handkerchief and wipes her hand first before imprinting his lips.[37] To lend authenticity to the saloon scene of In Old Chicago, King surmised that there would probably have been a team of German comedians: he was able to find Rice and Cady to perform the routine they did with him on the same bill in 1910.[38] As King once pointed out, "a director must be an inventor, the same as a writer. He must be able to take life and invent things that surround incidents and make [those incidents] human."[39]

When King talked about his work as director, two subjects surfaced again and again. To summarize once more, the first is the importance of the story. The story must be told clearly, and it has to be told by someone--that is the director's chief function. The actors must then understand the story and the characterizations which move the plot. It is therefore essential that the actor's interpretation be in harmony with the director's. A picture is in trouble when an actor goes off on his own story, or, as King would say, "goes out in left field."

The second element which recurs in King's discussion is that of mood or feeling. A picture is composed of scenes. For each scene the director must establish a prevailing psychological attitude; this mood, or feeling, becomes the key in which the scene is played. Here the collaborative nature of the medium is particularly evident, for setting, whether of landscape or of interior, is a visualization of the psychology the director wishes to suggest as he tells his story. "The background isn't something to look at. It's a feeling you try to get over."[40] Thus King pointed out that "if I have a situation where you want to show loneliness, instead of a person standing outside saying, 'I'm alone,' I get a long shot of a room, or whatever it is, with this person standing very small out here." (One thinks of Mae Marsh as the abandoned mother sitting at the end of a large public room in Over the Hill, or Peck as King David alone on his balcony looking out over Jerusalem; or Peck as the gunfighter standing apart from everyone else in the vast interior of the Gem Saloon.)

Obviously the art director and the wardrobe designer also make critically important contributions to the establishment of that mood. King would personally approve, or reject, each detail of their work. He might remove the ruffles which Charles Le Maire had added extravagantly to the Spanish matron in Captain from Castile, or reject Le Maire's design for Colbert's schoolteacher dress in Remember the Day. King knew the way a street lamp would look like in quattrocento Florence (Romola) or a side-wheeler steamship in the Victorian era. When In Old Chicago was being prepared, King remembered from his boyhood a picture of a locomotive of that time hanging in the office of J. W. Cook, a division superintendent in the Norfolk and Western offices; he was able to sketch the engine down to the brass fittings.[41] He found a beautiful field of tall oats for Anna and David in Way Down East, and against the advice of his Technicolor consultant, he insisted on retaining the vibrant reds of a cherry orchard--a splendid effect in Ramona.[42] King also contributed an important special effect for the fire sequence of In Old Chicago: he noted that the fire would appear hotter if shot against the sun's rays, and had Fred Sersen arrange the fire accordingly.[43]

King emphasized the critical importance of the cameraman. "There is an atmosphere, a feeling, a mood for every scene.... You're sort of painting with light," King recollected.[44] In addition to lighting the scene, the cameraman of course must photograph the shot from the appropriate angle or perspective. To those familiar with his work, the look of a Henry King film derives notably from the detached observation implicit in the medium shot. As Jean-Luc Godard once said, every shot is a moral statement. Distance offers the opportunity for objectification; a close-up for identification. King's medium shot suggests an attitude toward life which is contemplative, unsentimental, balanced and calmly observant. Although King worked with some of the greatest cameramen--he made three films with Henry Cronjager, two with Arthur Edeson, five with John Seitz, three with Hal Mohr, six with George Barnes, and two with Arthur Miller--none

The loneliness of age: Mae Marsh in Over the Hill (1931).

of these collaborations was as personally rewarding as his long-time relationship with Leon Shamroy, whose style is said "to have dominated production quality at Fox."[45] A visitor on location in Mexico reported of King and Shamroy that the two ate, drank, and slept pictures.[46] After King's second marriage, the Kings and the Shamroys (Mrs. Shamroy is the actress Mary Anderson whom King in 1944 had directed in Wilson) travelled and spent much time together while the men worked on pictures.

King was pleased to report that Shamroy knew his director well enough to "beat him to the punch...."

> A good cameraman is always trying to think... in terms of how you [as director] would tell that [some scene or event in the story].... Cameramen, good photographers, are dramatists also. When they light a set, they light it in the mood you're playing it in. A good cameraman has that sensitivity. He's studied the story and he's studied you. Shamroy was a man who would never leave the set without rehearsing."[47]

Just as a carpenter must know the tools of his trade, a director needs to understand the camera. "A camera is to a director," King pointed out, "as a hammer and saw are to a carpenter. A camera must talk."[48] The harmony between the two craftsmen is exemplarily illustrated in King's recollection that they used to work so well together that he called Shamroy a director and Shamroy called King a cameraman.[49]

But such close harmony was not always the case in King's work with other cinematographers. He admired Charles G. Clarke's photography, especially his exteriors. But Clarke on occasion had his own ideas about how to shoot a scene and how to impart glamor. In Margie (1946), Jeanne Crain is coming the first time to her father's place of business, an undertaking establishment. King had asked James Basevi, his art director on the picture, to design a funeral parlor with two long cathedral windows. He wanted a green spot on a casket, but Clarke couldn't understand why King wanted such an eerie look in a musical. When King arrived on the set the next morning, he saw the cathedral windows were streaming bright light. King asked Clarke to cut the light down, to light it so as to get a spiritual quality, with the assistant undertaker entirely in silhouette. Clarke couldn't understand and protested, so King shot the scene Clarke's way (as he would occasionally do rather than argue). Then King shot it as he wanted it. That evening when the rushes were shown, King's scene came across as very funny--a moment of comedy in a funeral parlor.[50] King also remembered a conflict when Clarke lit up a set where Margie was studying--"Lights and lights and lights." King pointed out that wasn't what he wanted. Clarke, of the old school, replied, "Well, I've got to make women beautiful." That was the sort of aesthetic choice which in King's mind threw the scene out of character. It was a different concept of the narration. Shamroy, by contrast, "was always in the mood of what you were doing."[51] On the same picture, Margie is in the bathtub singing "April Showers." King arranged for light bubbles--not soap bubbles but the bouncing kind used to test air currents in wind tunnels--to float around her as she is taking her bath. Clarke wanted to play colored lights upon them. King objected that the colors would be "gilding the lily" as each one contained the full spectrum. King boasted that he got a production number for a quarter.

Despite his insistence on the collaborative nature of the medium, King's personal contribution must not be undervalued. It is worthwhile to examine how decisions were made at Fox during the Zanuck regime. Zanuck was the nerve center of the studio. He personally assigned every script, whether complete or in process, to a director. Sometimes King would ask for the assignment, as he did for Jesse James and Remember the Day. (On rare occasions he would not get approval, as when The Robe [1953] was assigned to Henry Koster.)

King would customarily take the script and fly away for a week or two to Florida or some resort and hole himself up in seclusion. He would pore over the script, always keeping in mind the advancement of the story. Sometimes he had worked with the writer on the screenplay (as he had worked with George Hobart in 1923 on The White Sister; with Sonya Levien on State Fair and The Country Doctor; with Philip Dunne on Stanley and Livingston; and George Seaton on The Song of Bernadette.) By the time the shooting script was prepared King's contributions--changes, additions, revisions--were significant.

A study of King's recollections of his pictures in the Oral History Project will show how extensive these contributions could be. Here are a few: King

*added the love-interest and tripled the Hatburn antagonists in Tol'able David.

*made Stanley of Stanley and Livingston a hard-boiled journalist instead of an idealist.

*concocted the collision of Fulton's steamboat into the pier in Little Old New York.

*eliminated the vision of the Virgin from George Seaton's screenplay in which she appeared 17 times.[52]

*cut the ending from Wilson and pared Deep Waters to the bone.

*revised the troubled script of Twelve O'Clock High and suggested flashbacks (with no dissolves: at that time a technical innovation) for The Snows of Kilimanjaro for which he approved an upbeat ending.

*provided the motivation for the Methodist preacher in I'd Climb the Highest Mountain.

*received Hemingway's personal approval for the revised script of The Sun Also Rises (despite Hemingway's later denial).

*completely re-wrote the plot of The Bravados to demonstrate that vengefulness is a terrible mistake.

That his work with writers incurred their deepest admiration is well attested. Philip Dunne pointed out that

> Henry's method was to spend many weeks with the writer, painstakingly going over the script again and again until he was completely briefed on every nuance the writer had in mind. You could call it rehearsing without the actors, and certainly the psychology of every character was explored.

Dunne observed that when he himself began directing, he sought the qualities he had observed in the three great directors he had scripted for: Wyler, Ford, and King.[53] George Seaton, who greatly admired King's work for Bernadette, thought him "the most underrated director in the films" and "one of the greatest."[54] In a Christmas letter to King, Lamar Trotti wrote of the pleasure and profit in their long friendship and collaboration, and of his anticipation of the promise of further work together (December 16, 1944). Beirne Lay, Jr., co-author of the novel and scenarist with Sy Bartlett of Twelve O'Clock High, said of King's contribution: "All Henry did was take our novel and our screenplay and come up with a picture that was better than either. How many writers have made that statement?"[55] Nunnally Johnson considered that King's "experience, his knowledge, his intelligence, his sense of drama were pure gold. He has not received nearly enough credit for his accomplishments. If Ford's record is better it is only by the slightest margin. None of the others come anywhere near Henry King."[56]

After the script was assigned to a director, Zanuck would sit down with him and the writer, and, if Zanuck were not personally producing, the associate producer. King explained the efficiency of the process and the authority of the director:

> Twentieth-Century Fox had an awfully good budget system. You sat down in a room planning a story. After the script was pretty well finished, the director sat down and the assistant sat by him. You had the head of transportation, you had the head of the art department, the set department, the head of the men's

> wardrobe, the head of the women's wardrobe. When each of these people worked out what their budget was, and what they thought, the director had to answer all their questions. Sometimes the associate producer was there, but none of these questions could he answer.... The associate producer could convey messages from one person to another, or assign some preparation. But Zanuck looked straight to the director for everything; he didn't expect a lot from the associate producer.[57]

Joseph Behm,[58] King's production manager on many of his pictures, supplemented this pre-production procedure with the following account. King would first work with the writer on a screen play, injecting from time to time his interpretation of the story...

> After months of hard work, he would get the story the way he wanted it, for you must realize, he is the one who has to tell the story, and no one else. After this phase has been completed, he would start on the casting, make tests of the people he wanted for the parts, from the Stars to the bits. After this was done, he would decide on a starting date for the picture, depending on the availability of players. He would then give his production manager (me, on most cases) a script and say, "Let me know what you think?" After reading it, if I had any suggestions, we would discuss them. If not, he would instruct me to break it down and put it on the board (crossplot). He would determine the length of time the picture would take, the locations, the amount of extra players we would need, and the cost of the picture.

Behm recalled that it was at this point King had scripts sent to departments so that at a staff meeting the art director, Lyle Wheeler or one of his designates, could display plans and models of the sets, and the other departments (camera, wardrobe, property) could also make their presentations. King would outline as precisely as possible his expectations. He would explain how he was going to shoot the picture. At the end of the two- or three-day meeting, there was no doubt in anyone's mind as to what King wanted.

Behm recalls what happened next: "The next step would be to tie down the locations. If it was a domestic assignment he would take his own airplane." On foreign flights King would book a commercial airline, taking his art director and production manager. There were logistical questions to consider: how far must the crew travel every day? Would local people cooperate? What would be the cost of housing, transportation, and food?

"But even after shooting is completed," Behm continued, "the task for Mr. King is only beginning. He must edit the film. Will it work?" With King it works, Behm reflected "because he knows every phase of making a successful motion picture."

Behm then recalled King's final phase of production:

> After the picture is edited, he turns it over to the music department. He instructs the Composer [as to] the type of music he wants, and where. This done to his satisfaction, he then runs the finished film for his staff. After this, he orders the necessary prints, and usually says, "Ship it."[59]

And even then King did not think of his work as complete. In 1921 he personally toured Tol'able David, presenting the film in different parts of the country.[60] In 1936 King devoted time to marketing The Country Doctor, taking it to exchanges across the country and to studio-arranged meetings with key exhibitors. When Zanuck wondered why he was doing this, King replied that it was all part of the service. Zanuck was so impressed that he raised his salary $25,000 a year--at a time when a single-engine private plane cost $9,000.

For King such work was play. And play it is if one recalls that in English and German, to play is to imitate an action, and thus games and drama may be linked as an imitation of life. King worked a 12-hour day, was on the set at 7:00 a.m., rarely sat down, and delighted in his vocation. He never tired of the constant challenge:

> To make a picture, you work for months preparing a story, going into business, getting a crew, getting a staff, getting sets built, doing research. You complete the picture--you edit it--you preview it--you're out of business. Now you start over and go into an entirely new business. You have only the experience and judgment gained from past performances. You can't use anything... from this past picture. You can't use the same technique or anything else because it doesn't fit--like trying to wear another man's clothes.[61]

As a thoughtful, sometimes critical, often affectionate observer of the American scene, King created five of his finest motion pictures on American themes or in American settings. To observe his movement from film to film, his responses from decade to decade; to examine how he revealed, perhaps quite unconsciously, his sense of the American promise as well as his sense of its frustration, and of its expectations thwarted by the rise of industrialism and urbanization as the century advances: these are the concerns of the present critical work. But to see the world as Henry King saw it, it is necessary first to understand the world from which he emerged, for to some extent every artist writes his autobiography.

NOTES

1. Kevin Brownlow and John Kobal, *Hollywood: The Pioneers* (Alfred A. Knopf: New York, 1979), p. 10.

2. See Richard Cherry, "Henry King: The Flying Director," *Action* (July/August 1969): 6-8.

3. Dwight Macdonald, *On Movies* (Prentice Hall: Englewood Cliffs, 1969), pp. 86-88.

4. Frank Capra, *Frank Capra: The Name Above the Title: An Autobiography* (MacMillian: New York, 1971), p. 246.

5. It must be admitted, however, that there are occasions when it is not clear whose story King is telling. The spy-melodrama *The Woman Disputed* (1927) may be troubled for the same reason as the glossy *I Loved You Wednesday* (1933), both films which share directorial credits with others. The chief problem of the beautiful but flawed *Chad Hanna* (1940) is Nunnally Johnson's spotty script. *This Earth Is Mine* (1959) is dismally long, and it is never clear whether the script is about the earth, wine-making, Rock Hudson/Jean Simmons, or his majesty Claude Rains. Nor is it ever certain whether the story of *Beloved Infidel* (1959) is Scott Fitzgerald's or Sheilah Graham's.

6. Henry King at Claremont, videotape, 1977.

7. Ibid.

8. Ibid.

9. Ibid.

10. Ibid.

11. Joe Hyams, New York *Herald-Tribune* (February 13, 1958).

12. Cynthia Kirk, "Pioneers '73," *Action*, 7 (November/December 1973): 29.

13. Letter to Larry Bradley, October 16, 1974.

14. February 14, 1972.

15. Oral transcripts of Henry King to Ted Perry, p. 343. The author gratefully acknowledges Mr. Perry's graciously making available these materials. Subsequent citation(s) is to Perry.

16. Perry, p. 65.

17. Studio Press Release for *Maryland*, 1940.

18. "I'll never forget him! Never!" Franklyn Moshier, *The Films of Alice Faye* (San Francisco, 1978), p. 6.

19. Except where otherwise indicated, biographical information is taken from King's Oral History conducted for the Director's Guild of American, David Shepard, Interviewer. Hereafter referred to as Oral History.

20. Gene Phillips, *Hemingway and Film* (Frederick Ungar: New York, 1980), p. 131.

21. Perry, p. 72.

22. Janet Gaynor. Telephone interview with the author, November 25, 1983.

23. Jean Peters. Interview with the author, November 16, 1983.

24. Ralph Bellamy. Letter to Larry Bradley, ca. 1973, in which Bellamy remembered his role in The Woman in Room 13 (1932).

25. Letters to Larry Bradley, ca. 1973.

26. Perry, p. 673.

27. King recalled that George Stevens' way of working was to talk quietly with an actor; never to point, punch or drive hard. Ford would maneuver an actor into the same understanding of a role he had. See Perry, p. 570.

28. Perry, p. 318.

29. Perry, p. 242.

30. Perry, p. 101.

31. Oral History.

32. "Director Is Patient," Los Angeles Examiner, December 3, 1960.

33. Perry, p. 583.

34. Quoted by Tom Stempel, Screenwriter: The Life and Times of Nunnally Johnson (A. S. Barnes: San Diego, New York, 1980), p. 93.

35. Henry King. Interview with the author, August 14, 1981.

36. Perry, p. 222.

37. Perry, p. 7

38. Studio Publicity Release, In Old Chicago, 1937.

39. Oral History.

40. Hyams, op. cit.

41. Studio Publicity Release, In Old Chicago, 1937.

42. Oral History.

43. Oral History.

44. Perry, p. 18.

45. [q.v.] Ephraim Katz, The Film Encyclopedia.

46. Hyams, op. cit.

47. Oral History.

48. Roy Pickard, "The Tough Race," Films and Filming 42 (September 1971): 41.

49. Perry, p. 205.

50. Perry, p. 455.

51. Oral History.

52. Contrary to Leonard Moseley's account in Zanuck: The Rise and Fall of Hollywood's Last Tycoon (Little, Brown: Boston, 1984), pp. 218-219. It was Zanuck who asked King to let the audience see something of what Bernadette saw.

53. Letter to Larry Bradley, n.d., ca. 1973.

54. Ibid.

55. Letter to Larry Bradley, October 25, 1973.

56. Letter to Larry Bradley, November 16, 1973.

57. Perry, p. 115.

58. Behm was master property man from 1935 to 1942. His duties were to break a script down to determine what would be needed for set dressing--buggies, wagons, guns--whatever was not the responsibility of the art director or wardrobe. (Behm explained that "every prop must be backed up by pictures and research before it is submitted to the Director for his approval.") Behm became assistant director on The Song of Bernadette in 1943 and worked at this level until 1949, at which time he was promoted to production manager. He remained in this position until his departure from Fox in 1956. Later he became executive production manager to John Wayne until his retirement in 1970.

59. Letters to Larry Bradley, n.d., ca. 1973.

60. The writer interviewed a Blue Grass resident who in 1921 was living in Ohio and vividly recalled his presentation of the region--and the natives in the picture--as some exotic kind of Americana.

61. Perry, p.8.

Dressed for Success: The dapper director about to board his new roadster. Henry King was noted for sartorial elegance and predilection for automobiles and airplanes.

Chapter 2
The Road to Hollywood

The King family had been in Virginia for four generations when Henry was born in 1886. Henry's grandfather, John Howell King, was one of five brothers who had served in the Army of the Confederacy; he was a man whom his grandson remembered as being categorical in his judgments: "right was right and wrong was wrong."[1]

Henry's father Isaac was a hard-working farmer who seems to have done well despite depressed farm prices in the 1890s. He owned his land and farmed about 800 acres, some of which he leased. Henry's mother, in the words of her grandniece who remembers her well, was a gracious woman who set a good table, and raised ducks and chickens. She was a devoted mother.[2]

The community of Elliston, in which they lived, was only two miles from Christiansburg in Montgomery County and seems to have been populated by hard-working, church-going citizens and was relatively free of gossip or scandal, as King recollected 70 years later. The family attended the Methodist church, said grace before meals, and knelt for evening prayers before bed.

There were many chores for Henry and Edward, his elder brother by three years. The boys learned to work with machines, for Isaac Green was a man who liked machinery, and his sons enjoyed studying how things worked. There were also animals which the boys helped take care of. One winter, when the snow was deep enough to cushion falls, Henry took a colt from the stable and learned to ride bareback--a practice which would later prove useful when he made his living as a cowboy actor.

It was evidently a secure environment for a growing child. He received his education at a little blue schoolhouse on the banks of the Roanoke River. At an early age Henry showed a keen interest in stories. When he was finishing the seventh grade, he prepared a recitation which so engaged the audience of students, teachers, family, and all others attending an important community event that the principal teacher of the school, Mr. Jim Graham, sought Henry's mother out after the ceremony to make an unusual prediction: "Tonight's performance just may change this boy's entire life. I see him going in this direction; I mean he has a sense of the entertainer, a sense of the dramatic." It was as if a seed were there, and Graham's words were the water that nourished the germination.

At that time in America every part of the country was visited, at one time or another, by some kind of travelling entertainment. In 1906, there were as many as 300 touring companies.

There were also Uncle Tom companies, minstrel troupes, and for little villages and bywaters, medicine shows.[3] At the turn of the century, Christiansburg would have been large enough to attract a touring minstrel (at that time whites in blackface, or "Ethiopian" minstrels), if not a larger troupe. It certainly attracted a medicine show. Medicine shows typically featured a flashy huckster accompanied by two or three assistants with banjos. They would offer songs, dances, and comic turns as a lure to bring the crowd to hear the huckster's rhetorically extravagant hokum on the virtues of some bottled remedy guaranteed to cure in man or beast an astonishing range of ailments. (In a movie, the huckster was the kind of part Guy Kibbee could effortlessly play, a role he approximated as the struggling circus owner in King's Chad Hanna [1940]).

One such trouper, a Dr. Alward, so enthralled King when he was about 12 that he stayed on after the show to talk to this man who seemed like such a glamorous figure. Alward was no doubt stimulated by the responsiveness of the boy. He talked on describing the exciting adventures of the open road. The boy drank it all in so readily that Alward realized that here he might have a promising assistant. Would Henry like to join the show? He could find a place in his company for a young man willing to work. Henry was sufficiently tempted to give the prospect some consideration before realizing that there were other things for him to do with his life. For one thing, there was talk in the family of his going eventually to the University of Virginia. His marks in school were high, and several relatives had attended that institution. For another thing, from time to time Henry's family had mentioned the ministry to him, and he had thought about a vocation in the Methodist church.

Eighteen ninety-eight was an eventful year for the 12-year-old. His brother Edward, eager to work in the industry whose machines were transforming America, had left home at 15 to find employment in Roanoke, a raw young city that owed its existence to the junction of the Norfolk line from the seacoast with a railway line to the West. A happy event that year for Henry was the birth of his baby brother Louis, for whom he developed immediately a solicitous regard. He was happy, secure in a strong family, doing well in school, with prospects for the University. Later in the year, Henry's father died suddenly of a heart attack. With his father's death, all of Henry's plans for the future had to be revised. Obviously there was no one old enough to run the farm, and there was another mouth to feed.

But in Roanoke, Edward was doing well in his new work, having found a place in the Norfolk and Western. After having won the confidence of his superiors, Edward suggested that Henry come to Roanoke and live with him; he, too, could find a job with the Norfolk and Western.

More than any other application of land-based steam technology, the great locomotives symbolized the power of the new age; they would shrink the distant stretches of an agrarian society. In the Roanoke train yard of the Norfolk and Western, Henry watched the long trains connect Virginia with the far-flung cities of the huge country. In the trainmaster's office he studied the framed prints of famous locomotives. He began as a callboy but after a while his jobs were so varied that he "was everything imaginable around the railway center." Additionally he began taking courses in what he later thought was rather fancifully termed "combustion engineering." Edward, on the other hand, began applying himself to the study of diesel technology, in which field he would ultimately find his fortune.

Among the opportunities such a city as Roanoke could offer were touring companies which played weekly at the theatre. Henry and Edward went often to such entertainments; but Henry hardly allowed himself to think seriously of a career in acting. Never far from his consciousness, however, were Mr. Jim Graham's words; Graham was at least one person who could see him somehow entertaining crowds just as the travelling players were doing all over the Eastern seaboard. One attraction of that life was that players were constantly on the road, constantly exposed to new places and people. If acting as a career might not be realistic, the railroad could nevertheless offer him the opportunity to travel.

Henry worked for the Norfolk and Western for five years. He was strong, able, and eager to see the world. In 1904 he decided to lie about his age; that year he got his first job as a locomotive fireman. The following year, ready to leave Virginia, he sought and secured a job on the most important line on the Eastern seaboard, the New York Central; in this work he travelled the Midwest, for he was headquartered in Cincinnati. Meanwhile, Edward was demonstrating a new device in locomotive technology, the Kincaid Stoker, and Henry, having studied the device, lectured about it to assist his brother.

By 1906 Henry found himself in Indianapolis. With some time on his hands, and because it was never his nature to be idle, he decided to apply himself to a strange and improbable interest. Stimulated by the hours he had spent watching vaudeville in the halcyon days of that entertainment (born a mere 25 years earlier), King asked to be instructed in tap-dancing. His teacher was Professor Raynor (or Rayno). Little is known of this period in King's life except that he was diligent in application, if not especially skillful in his accomplishment. He was certainly personable and attractive, and at 6'4" with a clear and healthy complexion, Raynor realized that Henry would make a striking figure on the stage. Raynor spoke to his friend Carlos Inskeep who was organizing his own theatrical troupe to tour small cities the size of

West Salem and Bedford, Indiana. Inskeep called it rather grandly The Empire Stock Company. Carlos found Henry very taken with the idea.

But Henry had misgivings about leaving his career on the railroad, and he hated the idea of quitting. He decided that he would try it both ways: he would ask for a leave of absence during which he would test the waters of his new calling. He wrote his mother back home that he was changing jobs and joining The Empire Stock Company. His mother received the news quite comfortably: she thought he was joining an investment firm. What Henry did was all right with her. So in 1906, at the age of 20, Henry embarked on a career in which change was the only constant.

The tradition of "life upon the wicked stage" was still current throughout the country, but especially in middle-class homes and in strongly Protestant environments. Vaudeville as a "clean" entertainment for respectable audiences had been inaugurated in the early 1880s; before this time, performers had had to act in saloons and beer halls. Many actresses in such entertainments were of easy and vendible virtue, just as the comics were raucous and salty. Hence there was a distrust of entertainment among pious folk, which in some areas of the South would extend even to such innocent pastimes as music. To cite one instance (ca. 1885), a Presbyterian minister (also a schoolmaster) in Floyd County, not far from Montgomery, was forced to put away his violin after protests from his congregation.

It may then be surmised what reaction would come from Henry's father's family--who were strict and Methodist--when it was learned that Henry was not pursuing a career in investments. Three months after Henry had joined the Empire Stock Company, his father's sister confronted Henry's mother with the news after church one Sunday. Henry had run away with a troupe of players! The sister thanked God that his father was not alive to see this disgrace! But Mrs. King valiantly defended her son's choice, despite her sister-in-law's indignation. Family feeling was so strong that the two women were never to speak to each other again.

In his new career Henry was learning rapidly, as he did in everything that he undertook. He learned as a fledgling actor that at 20 years of age it is difficult to know what life is like at 30 or 50. But he was handsome on the stage, quick in his responses, skillful with his hands, tireless in application, friendly and direct with everyone, and happy to help in any situation. Most importantly, he had no ego problems to stand in the way of his learning.

He learned roles in his repertory of nine plays. His schedule required all the energy at the disposal of a young man, for typically in a week there were six evening performances and three matinees. He had to do more than perform; he had to assist in the numberless tasks attending production. In early manhood he knew the value of collaboration. His company could make do with very little. Theaters in the largest towns where his company toured were typically equipped with three settings: a drawing room (or "center door fancy"), a forest, and an olio drop, a curtain in front of which a miscellany of comic routines and musical turns could take place. King observed the ingenuity with which a troupe could accommodate six plays to what were basically two sets. The Empire Stock Company carried no sets, only a couple of dye drops.[4]

For the next few years, Henry moved from company to company and played in a variety of productions. One was Uncle Tom's Cabin--a seemingly inexhaustibly popular piece (in 1906 there were 13 companies touring the show), so that anyone in the habit of going to the theatre must have seen the play more than once. He played Broadway melodramas--mystery thrillers like Meredith Nicholson's The House with a Thousand Candles (will the hero survive the ordeal of spending a night in a spooky house to satisfy the terms of a will?); romantic love stories like The Common Law (sacrificial love and an artist's life set contemporaneously in exotic Paris); and romances like G. B. McCutcheon's Graustark (a fresh-faced and energetic young American chases a mysterious princess to her European kingdom where he helps foil scheming revolutionaries and at the end claims her for his bride).[5]

But Henry also had a chance to extend himself in unforeseen ways when he met a woman whom he was always to speak of after with a certain reverence: Anna Boyle Moore, an actress who had once played in classical theatre. Henry studied Romeo; he studied Orlando; he probably studied Brutus or Marc Antony. He may not have known what he was reading, but patiently Anna Boyle Moore would work with him until he understood what he was saying. He was never to forget her and the gift of her tutelage.

Additionally King mastered a blackface song and dance specialty for his "olio." By this time he could do a passable buck-and-wing as well as minstrel numbers, which were vastly popular entertainments. As an olioist in another routine--such was the mentality of the times--he donned a black stocking and fell on his knees. On stage right a white man would appear cracking a whip. "Come here, Tom, you black devil; you belong to me body and soul!" King would reply: "Yes, I know my body may belong to you, but my soul...." The other man would say, "What of your soul?" King would reply, "My soul belongs to the Ajax Brewing Company!" Blackout.

As a novice actor his salary--and there were many times when he was not paid--was $9 a week. King threw himself into his work; as long as he had his room and board covered and enough laundry money to keep a fresh shirt and good tie and starched collar, he would not complain. The constant pressure of learning a new role was taxing, for sometimes he had only one or two days to prepare a part. He remembered one wintry night in Asheville: to keep awake at 3:00 a.m., he broke the ice on the wash basin to splash his face with water. Travelling over country roads provided other rigors. On one occasion the company, travelling in a four-horse omnibus, had to ford a flooded river. Sometimes they would travel by riverboat and play towns along the riverside, such as Uniontown and Paducah. When arriving at a new town, everyone would first scatter through the streets to distribute handbills, then they would rehearse; then came the evening's performance. King remembered that he was hardly able to see the towns they toured because of the extensive preparation, rehearsals, and performances. It was the hotel and the theatre; the theatre and back to the hotel, or perhaps more likely, a boarding house.

When he did find himself with some time, Henry always attempted to engage another actor in polishing a scene. "Let's see if we can do this any better," he would say. His hard work, courtesy, stamina, inexhaustible interest, and readiness to engage in every aspect of theatre--from selling tickets to painting scenery, from office work to stage-managing--paid off, so that by 1910 he had risen at age 24 to leading man status.

In some sense the theatre was King's higher education. It gave him discipline and it offered him training in music, comedy, melodrama, dance, minstrels, and even a little Shakespeare. King said that he worked several times harder preparing for roles than he would have at the university, sometimes studying until 6:00 a.m. and then going to rehearsal at 9:00 a.m. He found playing with the Osmond Stock Company especially beneficial, for there were people who had been actors for over half a century who shared their knowledge with him. Among the companies he played in were the Commonwealth Company and the Mason-Newcombe Company. The Jolly American Tramp Show, run by his old friend Carlos Inskeep, toured for months in the Dakotas and Minnesota. His companies became more established and less transient at a time when theatrical attendance was generally declining and the competition was becoming more intense. (In 1911 there were only 250 companies, a loss of about 10 per year since 1906.)[6] Through the leading lady of the Jolly American Tramp Show, King came to know one of the big theatrical companies in Chicago, Rowland and Clifford, who offered him a part in Myron Leffingwell's _The Minister's Daughter_, and then he toured for several months in _The House of a Thousand Candles_, going as far as California.

When the College Park Theatre of Chicago was preparing _The House of a Thousand Candles_, King, as it happened, had just returned from this tour. He observed the new director fumbling for some solution to a directorial problem; King suggested that he could help with the appropriate business for the scene. The director sarcastically asked if King could direct the scene better. King innocently assumed that the question was sincere and took over. The director sat down and King quite by accident began to enter directing. He inadvertently assumed such duties again after Baker and Castle engaged him as Grenfall Lorry in Graustark. Baker instructed the company before it left New York that neither a jot nor a tittle of movement and business should change. But on the road King found that there were many ways to improve the show: it made sense, for example, to have Grenfall Lorry turn his back to the audience in the throne room. Despite Baker's firm instructions, King's changes registered such significant improvement that Baker accepted them--and congratulated King.

Henry's prospects were constantly improving, and at last he was going to have a chance to play New York, for the Henry W. Savage Company offered him the lead in a comedy called Top o' the Morning. Henry was on the verge of accepting when an incident occurred which, despite its apparent accidental character, would change his life forever.

When he arrived in New York, King was to have lunch with Helen Hamilton, the daughter of the owner of the Osmond Stock Company, from whom he had learned so much a few years earlier. His other companion was an actress who was going for an interview with a man about making moving pictures; her name was Pearl White. With nothing better to do, he walked with her to her appointment. He found himself standing in a crowded hall. Shortly thereafter, she emerged with a man whom she introduced to King as Mr. Wilbert Melville, a producer for the Lubin Western Studios in Pasadena. Melville sized up the tall, young actor (he was now 26) with the intense blue eyes and asked, "Why don't you go into motion pictures?" King told him that his blue eyes--so he had heard--wouldn't photograph. "Oh," Melville replied,"we fixed that years ago." Melville's question was an invitation, and so the motion picture career of Henry King was born.

King was struck by this chance encounter. He happened to accompany a friend; he happened to be waiting in a corridor; Melville happened to exit. Was such an event purely happenstance? Or was there, as he began increasingly to wonder, some destiny guiding him? Mr. Graham's prediction of Henry's future in dramatic entertainment still echoed in his ears: could that have been just an accident? And taking dancing lessons and meeting Carlos Inskeep: were these linked events of his own making or a result of fate?

King may not have known that Sophocles taught that character is fate. King's hard work and dramatic gifts may have created the destiny which meant making films. Certainly he felt himself strangely connected by a series of fortuitous events; in time he would realize that Henry King would be the connection for others: he would affect hundreds of acting careers; thousands of workers would, to some extent, owe their success to a studio he would help to save and to another studio he would help to create; millions would perceive the images he realized and would in some often imperceptible way be influenced by his philosophy. The philosophy which steadied him in his journey was shaped by his high-principled father and a devoted, loving mother, by a community of citizens who respected the church and the law, by Mr. Graham and the little blue schoolhouse. A small-town boy from Virginia would become the world's most successful contract motion-picture director.

But this success could not have taken place unless there was the character to make it possible. King had courage which enabled him to take a leap and enter a risky and marginal profession. He had the perseverance which kept him studying when, weary with fatigue, he would break the ice on his wash basin to study more. He had a lack of self-concern which allowed him to learn quickly and make play out of what for others might have been work. He had an innate courtesy which prompted him always to help. He had a sense of service which allowed him to put the benefit of the company before an immediate advantage. Most of all, he came to have a belief that he had been placed on the earth for a purpose.

Someone else came to assist that growing conviction. Again there was an apparent chance encounter which would turn out to be fully as important as Graham's words, Inskeep's invitation, and Melville's offer. When he was 37, King had scored two great successes in Tol'able David and 23 1/2 Hours Leave. Lillian Gish had chosen him, as had Barthelmess earlier, to launch her career as an independent star. The White Sister was to be the first post-WWI American production made in Europe; it would be shot entirely in Italy and North Africa. The crew was travelling aboard an American ship named, with an odd appropriateness, the Providence. Also aboard was a distinguished passenger travelling to the Vatican: Archbishop Bonzano who was about to be elevated to the cardinalate. Unlike the Protestant clergy in mountainous Virginia, the archbishop was a great lover of "photo-plays." One night in the Mediterranean beneath the stars he said: "You know, Henry, there are three great sources of knowledge in the world today--the Church, the University, and the Motion Picture. You have a great responsibility. You can reach more people than all the others. Sooner let a drop of poison fall into a glass of water than poison the minds of your audience." The archbishop's words carried the truth of recognition. Making films was a vocation. King might not have entered the Methodist ministry, but there was a way he could present life truthfully, holding the mirror up to nature, so that to use Hamlet's words, his work might show "virtue her own feature, scorn her own image." In some way every picture, as King realized, presents some model for behavior, and consciously or unconsciously, one is shaped by what one admires. King's films reflect courage, love, and dedication to something larger than personal advantage.

What then are the statements of value in a Henry King film? And to what extent are they embodied in the protagonist?

Typically, the protagonist of a King film is notable for inner resources which at times suggest spiritual depths. Two Tyrone Power vehicles are noteworthy. In Jesse James (1939), there is a contradiction in the role: the greater success he enjoys as a hero-bandit, the more estranged he is from what he really wants, which is a yearning for peace and family. In Prince of Foxes (1949), the hero discovers, despite his worldly success as a soldier of fortune, that there are some values he must be true to, and thus he renounces his spurious aristocratic claim to affirm the authenticity of his peasant origins (the mother, as in many King pictures, is here the agent of redemption). Gregory Peck is more characteristic of the King protagonist, although the muted pain born of introspection seems to be Peck's peculiar quality. One remembers his extraordinary recitation of the Twenty-third Psalm in David and Bathsheba (1951) with its deep longing for the spiritual communion which was his before the advent of Bathsheba. Ringo's stoic acknowledgement of his misspent life in The Gunfighter (1950) is not unlike Harry's misspent pursuits in The Snows of Kilimanjaro (1952) and Jim Douglas' in The Bravados. Warner Baxter (with whom King made two films) projected in One More Spring (1935) a combination of gentleness and compassion--similar characteristics to be found in all three of Ronald Colman's surviving vehicles: The White Sister (1923), Stella Dallas (1925), and The Winning of Barbara Worth (1926). Spencer Tracy is a high-minded government agent in Marie Galante (1934) and a dedicated newspaper reporter in Stanley and Livingston (1934), hardened by the demands of his profession but whose life is permanently transformed by the selfless practice and scientific research of the missionary doctor. Similarly, Jean Hersholt in The Country Doctor (1936) is a physician (significantly named Dr. Luke after the apostle of healing) who eschews a wealthy practice to labor for his fellow human beings in a distant Canadian village. President Wilson (Alexander Knox) envisioned the nations of the earth united in a parliament of the world, an idea for which he gave life (Wilson, 1944). In A Bell for Adano (1945), Major Joppolo (John Hodiak) risks his career to serve the Italian village he had been appointed to administer. One of King's favorite pictures, I'd Climb the Highest Mountain (1951), is the story of a Methodist circuit rider in the north Georgia mountains about 1910 who offers his service selflessly to his congregation. Not so spiritually motivated but nonetheless affected by a strong sense of civic idealism for his growing hometown is David Wayne's portrayal of a simple American barber in Wait till the Sun Shines, Nellie (1952). In Tender Is the Night (1962), Dick Diver sacrifices his career--and almost his life--to save the beautiful and unstable Nicole.

Emphatically, the statement in King movies is that one does not live for one's self. But there are other recurring motifs in his pictures. A person seems to be better equipped to face life if he lives in the country or a small-town. David Kinemon (Tol'able David) finds the support he needs from his mother and sweetheart in Greenstream, as well as the recognition of his elders. In the weighing of the agrarian past against an industrial future, the quality of life seems to tip the balance for the former rather than the latter. Although In Old Chicago (1939) beats the drum for the indomitable hog butcher of the world, in Wait till the Sun Shines, Nellie (1952), Chicago represents temptation and gangsterism. There is Norman Rockwell subject matter and nostalgia for the small town in I'd Climb the Highest Mountain. The Country Doctor opposes the characteristic virtues of neighborliness and a personal concern to corporate indifference and the specialist fragmentation of the city. The pastoral is the generic mode of such pictures as The Winning of Barbara Worth, Way Down East (1935), Ramona (1936), the racing picture Maryland (1940) and, perhaps, the dynastic wine-country melodrama This Earth is Mine (1959). The ambience of a small town and a salubriously concerned community are the contexts for the well-observed story of lobster-fishermen, Deep Waters (1948), and the charming musical Margie (1946), in which high school seems an especially pleasant place. Not so pleasant a place is the repressive and forbidding school of Remember the Day (1940), in which a censorious principal attempts vainly to blight the romance of the teachers. Booth Bay Habor in Maine is the colorful setting for the seaside community visited by a carnival in Carousel (1956).

If the protagonist in a King picture offers some kind of testimony to deep awareness and to the reality of love, truthfulness, and courage, there are other statements as well which may be inferred from the context of his films. One is that separation from significant social bonds is dangerous and destructive. The Greek and Elizabethan dramatists reiterate that isolation is tragic; in the films of Henry King isolation is often catastrophic. Certainly it is so for Stella Dallas when she is separated from Laurel. The isolation of Ringo is precisely the tragic problem in The Gunfighter (1950). King David is isolated once he allows the destruction of Uriah in order to give rein to his adulterous passion for Bathsheba. The poignance in Carousel (1956) arises from Billy Bigelow's revelation-from-the-past of his failure as husband and father.

Separation from the family--often from the mother--frequently constitutes the peripeteia in a King picture. The death of his mother provokes Jesse James' career as an outlaw. The death of Mrs. Wilson threatens the strength of the President during his turbulent office. The restoration of Lightnin' to his wife signals the comic finale in the film of that name (1930). When Johnny in Over the Hill (1931) goes to jail to save his father, the family disintegrates and his mother ends up in the poorhouse. When Alessandro is killed, Ramona is alone and destitute with her child, their happiness destroyed. The vengeful quest of Jim Douglas for his victims begins with the killing of his wife. The tragic situation of Tender Is The Night turns on Dick Diver's expulsion from his family by Nicole.

Family figures are pivotal in King's work. The mother is central and often the protagonist in such pictures as Salvage (1921), Tol'able David, Stella Dallas, Sonny (1922), The Winning of Barbara Worth, Lightnin', Over the Hill, Ramona, In Old Chicago, Jesse James, Maryland (1940), Prince of Foxes, The Gunfighter, and The Bravados (1958). The image of the Divine Mother is significantly present in Ramona, The Song of Bernadette (1943), and The Bravados. The father is conspicuously present in State Fair (1933), Carolina (1934), Wilson (1944), and Margie. Father figures, or men manifesting strong paternal regard, are notable in Deep Waters, Twelve O'Clock High (General Savage for his men) and Stanley and Livingston (Livingston for his African village).

When the family is not present, strong surrogate relationships bond people together in such a way as to suggest the reconstitution of the family. Thus in One More Spring (1935), the bankrupt antique dealer, the penniless "model," and the failed musician huddle together in Central Park against a bitter winter. Mary Ann tries to create a home for the temperamental musician she saves (Merely Mary Ann, [1931]); and Diane makes a "seventh heaven" in the garret for Chico the sewer cleaner in the film of that name (1937). The orphan in Deep Waters loves the lobster man--and wants to share his life aboard his boat, until he is frustrated by a social worker.

When the protagonist does not seek or find a family, it is because he or she has a higher purpose, a larger need to serve, sometimes a higher union to acknowledge. The preacher in I'd Climb the Highest Mountain serves his mountain congregation and is the agent for restoring a shattered family. Similarly, Dr. Livingston offers his life in Christian service, as Stanley, fired by his selfless example, dedicates himself as a bearer of light in journalism. The schoolteacher of Remember the Day follows her vocation with the same commitment the circuit rider brings to his flock in I'd Climb the Highest Mountain. The establishment of the Orange Free State is more important to van Riebeck than Katie

O'Neill's love in Untamed (1955). When her fiancée, missing in action, unexpectedly returns, the heroine of The White Sister does not hesitate to become the bride of Christ rather than the bride of Giovanni; and Giovanni will later sacrifice his life to save a village.

King shared with most of his fellow directors in the old Hollywood a fundamentally comic view of life. The classical understanding of comedy is a happy ending. To be sure, the conventions of the studio often imposed such finales (as in the ill-fated Marie Galante), but King's films that give meaning to such abstractions as courage, truthfulness, and faith often celebrate those moments of union when love shines forth like the light of heaven, and the feeling is as true as sunshine.

Some of the happiest moments in King's motion pictures take place when the family comes together. One thinks of David Kinemon looking at a picture book while his mother sews and his father reads. There is the quiet happiness of Abel Frake, his wife, and his two children riding in their truck in the moonlight against the tall corn of an Iowa summer, while the radio plays some gentle 1930s-style music. There is the moment in Wilson when the President, unbending in the glow of the lamplight, takes off his pince-nez, and joins his daughters at the piano to sing "By the Light of the Silvery Moon." Twilight settles and the lamp is lit over the dining table; someone plays "In the Gloaming" on the harmonium and the Bartletts gather for supper: that is the moment of happiness in Way Down East. It is Margie at the school prom dancing with her father at last to "My Wonderful One." And there are some memorable three-shot finales which celebrate such moments: when the engineer of Barbara Worth, who has made the desert bloom like a rose, drives up to his villa where his wife and child joyfully embrace him; when David Kinemon, after his arduous journey, is lovingly comforted by his mother and his girl; when the mother of Over the Hill, rescued from the bleak poor house, is welcomed by her son and daughter-in-law; when Jesse, Zee, and their five-year-old embrace each other happily as they make plans to leave for California; when Jim Douglas and his child unite with his former sweetheart at the ending of The Bravados.

As he had observed to others, King told Ted Perry, "I like pictures to be upbeat. When you leave the theatre I like for you to feel better going out than you did coming in."

On the whole, King's pictures reflect that sense of upbeat optimism, born of a time when Americans were confident of their country and of the individual's opportunities to succeed. These attitudes are embodied in the ragtime and swing of those years, in a trust that somewhere there is a plan, and that happy endings have a "rightness" to them. At the same time, there is a darkening of vision. This study will examine how the nineteenth-century ethos of individualism (so triumphantly displayed in Tol'able David) is challenged by social forces beyond individual control: by class structures in Stella Dallas, by the march of industrialism in Jesse James. Finally, the vast sunlit spaces of the old West have shrunk to the chilly bleakness of a Southwestern hamlet, the only place left for the gunfighter to go in the film of that name. It is also true that King's last pictures either force the optimism (Wait till the Sun Shines, Nellie, This Earth is Mine) or fail to demonstrate it (Beloved Infidel, Tender is the Night). Yet, on the whole, there is a faith in America and in the family which is implicit in most of his work and which is clearly manifest in the affectionately observed State Fair.

This book, which is in part a response to Andrew Sarris' uncertain classification of King as a "Subject for Further Research,"[7] will examine King's major American films, detailing the circumstances of their production and offering commentary on their artistic and cultural significance. What makes King's work distinctive, as we have observed, are these characteristics: a set of values and personal experience that offer his films a fundamentally comic structure; his generously collaborative notions about the work of cast and crew; his own sense of the importance of the story and the scenes which advance the story; and his highly developed professionalism which served him as he worked in an astonishingly eclectic range of subjects. These are the attitudes which created the movies that entertained the country for four decades.

NOTES

1. Oral History.

2. Mrs. Mildred Blankenship, Lynchburg, Virginia (July 17, 1984).

3. Miriam Winston, The History and Development of Road Companies in Twentieth Century America, M.A. Thesis, Brooklyn College (June 1970). Illustration, p. 5.

4. Perry, p. 694.

5. The author wishes to acknowledge the kind assistance of Professor Jack Ravage of the University of Wyoming, whose help in sorting out the theatrical companies with which King was affiliated, the plays with which he toured, and the dates of his life during his theatrical career has been most valuable. Professor Ravage's information is based on conversations with King and theatrical research.

6. Winston, ibid.

7. Andrew Sarris, The American Cinema: Directors and Directions, 1929-1968 (E. P. Dutton: New York, 1968).

American Innocence: Richard Barthelmess in Tol'able David (1921)

Chapter 3
Tol'able David: An American Pastoral

There is a place called Greenstream. Only Greenstream is a country of the imagination: it lies in a gentle valley behind three great ranges of mountains. The skies seem to be bluer in Greenstream, it is always summer, and the country flows with sparkling streams bordered with wild mint. Soft mountain light bathes the valley, and meadows dotted with grazing sheep roll up to the wooded crests.

Despite the passage of 60-odd years, Greenstream still shines bright, its white houses and country stores and churches nestled in the pastoral landscape. In Henry King's Tol'able David, one can see Greenstream for one's self, a place that really exists; only on the map it is called Blue Grass.[1] One must travel to Monterey in Highland County, and then turn toward the West Virginia border on Route 640, passing small Victorian churches set amidst rolling farms. Having passed Hightown, shortly thereafter on the left, on the other side of split-rail fence, is an old cottage, now missing its stone chimney. That is the home of the film's central character, David Kinemon.

There are a few changes since 1921. The spring house, the wooden trough, and the lilac and wild cherry are gone. But the present owners, Mr. and Mrs. Kenton Rexrode, who live next door in a newer home, have kept the old weathered house to store hay and old farm implements.

The Rexrodes know the house well, and like every resident of the region, they have seen the picture several times. Mrs. Rexrode can point to the area where the kitchen scenes were filmed. Mr. Rexrode can recognize the place where David's father kept his flintlock. They point out that here is the parlor of the opening scenes. A sheepdog on the place looks like his counterpart, Rocket, who frolicked on the property over 60 years ago. The Rexrodes are amazed to learn that the interiors of the film were photographed, not here on this farm in western Virginia, but in the old Biograph Studios on 174th Street in the Bronx.[2]

The stories that fill us with the deepest sense of meaning, that connect us to something beyond in time and place, are invariably those that figure some universal truth: a fruit is tasted and the garden is forfeited, a beast is loved and he turns into a prince, a maiden is kissed and she is awakened into consciousness, a proud man isolates himself and terrible suffering ensues, a gentle youth faces a fearful adversary and defeats him against impressive odds. Stories of this sort are testimonies to experience; primal stories repeated again and again that are basic to the understanding of life. *Tol'able David* draws openly upon the David and Goliath myth; as we first see David Kinemon, he is studying the picture of the young shepherd confronting the menacing giant. As a boy he fleets the time carelessly, enjoying the pleasures of his youth and the green world.

The pastoral is a form born of nostalgia, the longing of one caught up in the complex life of the metropolis for a simpler time, where the care of sheep and the songs and play of shepherds are principal concerns, as may be seen in the work of its two most influential poets, Theocritus (ca. third century B.C.) and Virgil (70-19 B.C.). By the Renaissance the form was extended: now there were serpents in the garden; exotic adventures added complexity; there was also winter; and there was death, as in the Guercino painting that includes a skull and with the inscription "Et in Arcadia ego" ("Even in Arcady there am I"). But rural life is the essential subject of the pastoral, as a biographer of Frost has written, or--to quote the *Oxford Companion to English Literature*--"the essence is simplicity of thought and action in a rustic setting." And so it was in Virgil's Arcadia and Shakespeare's Arden.

The film *Tol'able David*, of course, is but one in a line of American pastorals. Hollywood has long supported the deeply felt American tradition that opposes the virtue of country life to the corruption of the city; that sentiment is reflected in such generic forms as gangster films, Westerns, and love stories that flower by streams, in orchards, in sylvan retreats. D. W. Griffith had appropriated the form in such films as *True-Heart Susie* and *The Romance of Happy Valley* (both in 1919). Charles Ray made a living playing the role of a country swain in such pictures as *Plain Jane* (1916), *Peaceful Valley* (1920), *An Old Fashioned Boy* (1920), *The Old Swimmin' Hole* (1921).

Tol'able David, however, is a radiantly clear exemplum of the form. A few instances clearly relate the film to this tradition. The Biblical David was, after all, a shepherd who played a lyre and composed songs. David Kinemon has no lyre or flute, but he plays his harmonica; one is reminded of Sir Philip Sidney's shepherd boy who plays his pipe as if he never would grow old. The opening title in this silent picture alludes to "the pastoral valley of Greenstream," shortly after which follow, in the convention of the form, "idylls" (Greek for "little pictures"): a cock crowing, a wild cherry in blossom; hot cakes and coffee; a swimming hole and evening prayers; trout-spearing and mumblety-peg. These are the images that evoke the country life surrounding David. As if to connect with a popular rustic tradition in American humor, when David loses his clothes at the swimming hole he jumps into a barrel. But the exposure is wholly innocent; not the faintest suggestion of prurience attaches itself to this image, perhaps the best-known in the picture. David's activities are bucolic pastimes:

he plays with his dog Rocket, looks lovingly at Neighbor Hatburn's granddaughter Esther (who, among her activities, herds cows), swings on a gate, and sits on a split-rail fence to fantasize about driving the mail himself and receiving the admiration of Esther (at which point the fence collapses, paralleling the collapse of his dream).

But Tol'able David is also a story about coming of age, or the initiation that signifies the passage from adolescence into adulthood. David longs to take his place in the community; but he is too young to be entrusted with driving the U.S. Mail, he is too young for a drink, for a cigar, for a pipe. His attempt to smoke makes Esther laugh. As his mother reminds him, he is her baby; nevertheless he is "tol'able, tol'able." So far the intention of the film is comic.

But, as the title has it at this point, "trouble like a dark cloud descended upon the peaceful valley of Greenstream." Three outlaws from the adjoining state invade the home of their Hatburn relatives. Desperate men, they quickly assume command of Esther and her grandfather in the terrorized home. Luke Hatburn attacks Allen, David's appealing elder brother, stomping him mercilessly so that he lies motionless in the dust. The mute grief of the Kinemons upon learning of Allen's life-long paralysis is followed by Hunter Kinemon's resolution to avenge his son's crippling. But under the stress of the decision Kinemon suffers a fatal heart attack--and now the dual burden of avenging his brother's injury and supporting his family falls upon David's young shoulders. At this moment an agonizing conflict develops--for David cannot do both. Honor and the code of the community require that the fugitive Hatburns, a law unto themselves, be punished; but his mother, now realizing that David must become the support of the family, pleads tearfully for her son to stay home. Like an anguished suppliant in Greek epic, she falls to the ground to clasp her son's knees.[3]

Reluctantly, David accedes to his mother's request, a decision which incurs the disapproval of the elders of the community for shirking a moral responsibility. Unable to manage the land they have been farming, the Kinemons sadly pack their possessions and move to the village, where Mrs. Kinemon will take in washing. David has now lost his home, his father, and Esther; and Allen has been invalided for life. Sweeping floors at John Galt's store seems the only future open to him.

One day, however, the mail carrier shows up too drunk to drive. A passenger on the "hack," as the vehicle is called, protests that he will miss his connection unless he can get to the depot. With no alternative, Galt (who is also the postmaster) turns to David who joyously seizes the opportunity which will allow him to show his mettle. He can take on a man's job. But an untoward accident occurs on the return trip: the mail falls from the carrier at the bend in the road. And Luke Hatburn, who espies the accident, steals the bag and removes it to his lair. David, frantic at the frustration of his dreams, retraces his steps and surmises that Hatburn has indeed absconded with the bag. When David enters the Hatburn's home and demands the mail, he is greeted by the amused contempt of the outlaws, the youngest of whom aims his pistol at him and shoots. When blood streams from David's shoulder, he explains, "I only wanted to nick his ear, but he moved." Esther, stricken with terror, flees from the house, and Luke--hesitating between finishing off David or taking care of Esther in some unsavory manner--goes after Esther. Left alone with the two outlaws, David gains control of the contest by using the revolver entrusted to him as an agent of the mails, thereby removing two of his antagonists. Esther has not fled very far, having fallen prey to the fainting which afflicts her every now and then as she staggers toward Greenstream. After the first collapse, Luke catches up with her and looms over her prone body; then he hears shots from the house. He'll take care of Esther later, we surmise, as he bounds back to the house.

The finale of the film builds masterfully to an excruciating tension as the camera crosscuts between David and Luke in a fight which even today is vividly convincing (King recalled that the actor playing Luke fell so hard his head dented the floorboards), and shots of Mrs. Kinemon chatting with her neighbors while she waits at the store ("Whatever can be keeping David?"). These scenes are interspersed with glimpses of Esther, exhausted, fainting, and convinced that the outlaws have killed David.

But David has not been defeated. Wounded though he is, he uses his slightness to advantage in his contest with the hulking Hatburn. The actual vanquishing of Luke is not shown; what we see is far more effective. The door swings open to reveal the ominous blackness, then closes, then opens, then closes, then opens once more to what in the tension seems longer than a count of five seconds. Then David emerges, dragging his wounded body to the waiting hack. At the village a posse is simultaneously forming to apprehend the outlaws when David, to the triumphant cheers of the community, swings into view. Tenderly he is lifted from the vehicle to be laid in his mother's arms. "David, you're wonderful," murmurs Esther. "I'm tol'able, just tol'able," says David, whose face is now framed by the solicitous and adoring countenances of Esther and Mrs. Kinemon.

In King's compelling vision of nineteenth-century America, the moral development of David is a central concern. David's triumphant return to Greenstream with the mail signals the completion of the ordeal that marks his passage to man's estate. That he should have risked mayhem and murder to bring back the afternoon mail leaves some contemporary audiences more amused than admiring, if not incredulous; but surely such responses comment more on our inability to transpose ourselves to another time than to any foolish simplicity in David's character. As King pointed out in speaking of how respect was accorded in his own birthplace, "People don't realize that in a small town... to drive the hack, to carry the U.S. Mail was a responsibility--the biggest responsibility there was." In a mountain fastness the mail carrier provided the link with the outside world, and upon him the community depended. "David's brother was a great hero in his eyes," remarked King.[4] Whatever his occupation, a hero serves his people; David's willingness to risk his life in the name of duty represents the virtues which developed the country.

Some years ago in a widely-read account of the shifts in American values, Charles Reich suggested that American culture in its first phase (denominated as Consciousness I) enshrined as essential to the spirit that created the country the values of duty, responsibility, industry, perseverance, and sacrifice. "In a new and vast land," Reich wrote, "reality centered on the truth of individual effort. America would prosper if people would prove energetic and hard-working. The crucial thing was to realize the individual energy."[5]

By the 1930s it was difficult to remake Griffith's blockbuster-melodrama of 1920, Way Down East (as King tried to do in 1935). Tol'able David would prove anachronistic for John Blystone who attempted a remake in 1931. Griffith and King were both born into pre-automotive America; they were both products of the South and the rural community. Their films could speak to old-fashioned values because these filmmakers believed them; and although Griffith could never move with the times, King was able to continue to make fine commercial, occasionally artistic, motion pictures because he had mastered, and sometimes innovated, the technique of the developing cinema. At the same time he remained at heart an interpreter of vanished America, and especially the America of his youth, as such pictures as Over the Hill (1930), Remember the Day (1940), The Gunfighter (1950), I'd Climb the Highest Mountain (1951), Wait Till the Sun Shines, Nellie (1952), and The Gift of the Magi (1952) were to show. As a storyteller--a word which sums up King's sense of his vocation--his duty was to make the film come to life by creating the atmosphere that makes the sense of place. King knew the wooded mountains of western Virginia. As a boy, he took part in those pastimes and activities the film lovingly portrays.

This sense of place is what the Soviet director and film theorist V. I. Pudovkin called "color."[6] Tol'able David evokes a feeling, which verges on poignance, of "that's the way it must have been." Summer afternoons when men and boys play marbles together; the fiddlers bowing away on their instruments at the village social; the congregating of townfolk awaiting the daily mail; the gathering of the family for evening prayers; the sharpening of knives and scrubbing of clothes; the celebration of a special event with a jug of local brew; the use of a flywhisk made from shredded newspapers at mealtimes; the bucolicism of winding lanes and old mills--these are the "idylls," or little pictures, in which King recalled the country he grew up in; they are the details that made for the atmosphere Pudovkin was to pay tribute to.

If the director is a storyteller, a film director--in King's view--must tell his story in pictures, whether the medium is silent or sound; therefore, when King was making silent movies, he tried to show approximately 90 percent of the action in pictures and about 10 percent in titles. In the 109 minutes (at 18 fps) of Tol'able David, there are only 29 titles. King observed that the director's work is to invent the atmosphere that makes for the feeling of real characters in a real place.

Up to the making of Tol'able David in 1921, King's directorial career had been steadily gathering momentum. When he had been working as actor as early as 1913, he had passed time between scenes by writing scripts. By 1915 he had experimented with editing techniques. By 1916, he had started directing Baby Marie Osborne in her highly successful pictures. As he travelled up the rungs from Lubin to Balboa, and from Balboa to American (where he directed Mary Miles Minter and the popular William Russell), he consolidated his position with each successive move, so that by 1920 he had come to the attention of Thomas Ince, probably the most successful, certainly the most efficient, studio head in Hollywood. Ince offered King a Mary Roberts Rhinehart story, 23 1/2 Hours Leave, and, depending on the success of the picture, the option of a contract. He instructed King to take "a couple of punks [Douglas Maclean and Doris May] and make them into stars"--and then left on vacation. King made the picture and contrary to studio policy at Inceville (now Culver City), King insisted on supervising the cutting. The studio executive deputed in charge during Ince's absence was furious at King's officiousness and refused to renew the option. The picture nevertheless became a runaway hit, making stars of Maclean and May, but leaving King, now without his option with Ince, at loose ends with no immediate work in sight.

At this point, Robertson-Cole, one of the successful independents quartered in New York, invited King to come at their expense to New York to discuss a contract. King refused their offer of expenses to insure his independence, but went to New York to explore the possibility of work. Robertson-Cole was impressed and offered King a contract; but the day that they were to cement this deal, financial panic seized the bank in which Robertson-Cole kept its funds, and Robertson-Cole had no choice but to back off. Nevertheless, King made films without a contract for this company for about a year.

During this visit, King had been introduced to Jim Williams with whom he played golf; as First National's head Williams had had the prescience to sign Chaplin for seven pictures. Williams introduced King to Charles Duell, a New York attorney. Duell wanted to form his own company, engagingly to be named Inspiration Pictures. Richard Barthelmess wished to make an independent bid for stardom using a property which Griffith was ready to sell, Joseph Hergesheimer's Saturday Evening Post serial entitled "Tol'able David." Would King do the story as Inspiration's first venture? Duell offered King a small capitalization fund--$250,000--which he would then expend as seed money in the production of seven pictures; the contract would run from July 1921 to December 1922. With no other prospect, King decided to accept the offer.[7]

Barthelmess was 27 in 1921, some 10 years older than the part which made him a star. Eight years earlier he had been graduated from Trinity College (in Connecticut). His mother's stage experience led her to become a voice coach for the famous Ukrainian actress Alla Nazimova (whose English, heard 24 years later in Escape, seemed hardly to have improved by such tutelage). Nazimova had been signed by Carl Laemmle to star in War Brides (1916), one of Universal's earliest big critical and popular success. Although she was a family friend, she could no doubt surmise that Barthelmess' cameo good looks were strikingly photogenic; her confidence was to assure him an important part in the picture.

With his dark eyes, ivory skin, and chiseled profile, he won parts with such established players as Anna Q. Nilsson and Marguerite Clark. It was Dorothy Gish, however, who chose Barthelmess to play opposite her in a series of successful vehicles, but his big break came when Griffith cast him against Dorothy's sister Lillian. After the sudden death of his juvenile lead Bobby Harron, Griffith searched for a replacement who could combine Harron's sensitivity with greater strength. Barthelmess promised such sensitivity and was, moreover, better looking: as Lillian Gish has said, Barthelmess had the most beautiful face of any man who ever went before the cameras.[8] First in Broken Blossoms (1919) and then in Way Down East (1920), the two radiated a luminous purity which still lights up the screen today. After these successes and his work in two minor Griffith pictures, Barthelmess decided to strike out on his own.

In 1921 this decision may have seemed foolhardy to some people in the industry, for that year witnessed the crack-up of two careers. Nazimova's Beardsleyan version of Salomé was a commercial disaster. Charles Ray, another actor who had specialized in the country swain roles of which Barthelmess' David is representative, sank irretrievably after producing The Courtship of Miles Standish. And the Selznick superstar Clara Kimball Young would shortly destroy herself in attempting to manage her own company. But Barthelmess knew that his following was growing; he knew also that he had acquired a good property in Hergesheimer's widely followed Saturday Evening Post serial, a work retelling the David and Goliath story in a mountain setting. Duell would produce Barthelmess' films through Inspiration Pictures.

King chose for his cinematographer the almost forgotten Henry Cronjager. What is observable in Cronjager's work (as seen even in the lamentable The Seventh Day) are a striking freshness and clarity, and especially memorable are the scenes of early morning. No one who has watched Tol'able David attentively is likely to forget the two-shot of Rose and Mrs. Kinemon as they hold out their arms to Allen's broken body; or the mute grief of Rose rocking in the darkened bedroom where Allen lies helpless. The eloquence of these shots makes title comment unnecessary. Cronjager's meticulous attention to detail won from one of his directors, Marshall Neilan, the epithet of "Wait-a-minute-Henry." King explained that just when the cameras were ready to roll, Cronjager would cry, "Wait a minute! See that piece of paper over there? If it moves, nobody's going to look at the actors."[9] The successful collaboration of King and Cronjager on this picture brought Cronjager back to work with King on two other Barthelmess films, The Seventh Day and Sonny.

For his scenarist, King secured Edmund Goulding, an Englishman who had sought his fortunes first on the New York stage and then in the rapidly growing film industry. King asked Goulding to do a treatment and to scout for locations in the Virginia mountains. Although Tol'able David would be a highly successful partnership for both of them, Goulding's relations with King were troubled by the fact that he objected to script changes King thought necessary. To declare responsibility for these changes, King added his own name under Goulding's in the credits for screen adaptation. When the film became a hit, Goulding complained to Harriet Underhill of the New York Herald that King was now depriving him of his due.[10] King's addition of Esther (the love interest) and the tripling of the Hatburn antagonists were, however, enriching contributions to the Hergesheimer story. Despite this disagreement, King and Goulding were to collaborate on The Seventh Day and Fury, both Barthelmess pictures of 1923. Goulding later became a notable director, remembered for the early Crawford in Sally, Irene, and Mary (1925), Garbo in Love (1927), the star-studded cast of Grand Hotel (1932), and Bette Davis in four of her most sympathetic roles.

It remained for King to gather a cast quickly, and with the help of Edward Small, a well-placed theatrical agent, King swiftly chose his players that summer in New York. At the Lambs Club he ran into George M. Cohan's stage manager, Lawrence Eddinger--whom King was to cast as John Galt, the storekeeper and landowner whose farm David's family live on. At the same club he also met "Drunk Jack" Dillon whose dramatic specialization won him his soubriquet: Dillon would double as a passenger in one scene ("the drummer") and the besotted hack driver in another. Walter Lewis, who had created the role of a drunken referee in a popular vaudeville sketch, would supply the role of the outlaw father. Ralph Yearsley, a young Australian, was cast as one of the outlaw brothers. Edmund Gurney, a British actor who had come to New York to support Mrs. Patrick Campbell in Pygmalion, would portray David's father, the hardworking tenant farmer. The role of the kindly grandfather whose home is terrorized would be taken by Forrest Robinson, who recently on Broadway had played a paternal role in The Fortune Hunter. David's mother was to be played by Marian Abbot, an abundantly maternal actress under contract to Frohman and Belasco. Patterson Dial, who had appeared recently in the Central Theatre productions Aphrodite and Princess Virtue, was cast to play David's sister-in-law in the poignant role of the wife. There remained three important supporting roles: David's girlish sweetheart, Esther; David's dashing elder brother Allen; and the archetypal villain of the piece, Luke Hatburn.

When King met Ernest Torrence, an operatic baritone who had been graduated from such distinguished institutions as the Edinburgh Academy of Music, the Stuttgart Conservatory, and the Royal Academy of Music, King examined him quizzically: "Mr. Torrence, you look more like a banker than an outlaw. Do you think you could play Luke Hatburn?" Torrence, nervous despite his stage and music-hall experience, had never appeared before a camera; he thought a moment and accepted the part. He need not have been apprehensive, for after the film opened Metro was so impressed with his screen potential that they sent a special automobile to fetch him from his train before it was to arrive at the Los Angeles station.[11] Torrence transplanted easily to Hollywood where he became a familiar figure in the British colony, basking in his successes in some celebrated pictures of the time. He played the drunken frontier scout in the first Western epic, James Cruze's The Covered Wagon (1923); Captain Hook in Herbert Brenon's widely-admired Peter Pan (1925); Uncle Pío in Charles Brabin's The Bridge of San Luis Rey (1929); and Moriarty against Clive Brook's Sherlock Holmes in the 1932 film of that name.

A young, strong-jawed actor with blue eyes and a big smile from Culpeper, Virginia, Warner Richmond had toured on the stage early in the last decade and acted with Henry King. His work in film found him mostly on the West coast where he played in largely undistinguished pictures: the roles he played then and until his career declined in the 1930s were athletes, policemen, cowboys, soldiers--often second leads but in the company of rising actresses such as Dorothy Gish and Bebe Daniels. Shortly after the release of War Brides in 1916, he found himself having tea with a lady who had moved from the East. Richmond remarked that he had admired the young male lead in War Brides. Did the lady (whose name was Mrs. Harris) know this young actor Barthelmess? he asked. "Yes," Mrs. Harris replied, "He happens to be my son."[12] In a few years Richmond found the opportunity to work with Barthelmess when King offered him the role of Allen, "the strongest man in the county," who is paralyzed for life by Luke Hatburn.

For David's sweetheart Esther, King recruited an ingénue with extensive experience in theater and film, Gladys Hulette. She had entered movies as early as 1907, and in 1909 she was to play in Hiawatha, the first motion picture made by IMP, Carl Laemmle's maverick production company formed to break the Motion Picture Patents' cartel. By 1914 she was featured in Thanhouser Pictures, and by 1917 she was playing in the company of Florence La Badie and Irene Castle at Pathé. Although Miss Hulette continued to work steadily in films until 1928, Esther was to be her most important role. Her porcelain complexion, long lustrous hair, and soulfully compassionate eyes suggested a delicacy which flapper styles were soon to make old-fashioned.

King got away with absurdly low salaries, promising his actors expenses and cool locations in the Virginia mountains while New York was sweltering in a July heat wave. Eddinger and Dillon were engaged for $35 a week; Abbott for $50; Torrence and Richmond for $200; Hulette for $400; and Barthelmess for $1200.[13] The cast boarded the train for a 10-hour ride to Staunton. From Staunton, they traveled for 48 miles over the three ranges of mountains in a convoy of vehicles to descend to Monterey.

Barthelmess dramatically recounted the journey to a reporter. "Never have any of us traversed such roads nor looked into such precipices as stared back at us gruesomely on that night. We were not altogether reassured when we saw our driver place in the car within easy reach a repeating rifle." The driver explained that on a recent journey two wildcats had jumped from the trees.[14]

The actors--so it was reported--arrived in Monterey with lights blazing, and the citizens of the community heavily armed in expectation of a visit from a band of local outlaws called the Ryder boys. Barthelmess exaggerated when he claimed that the company "found primitiveness that could not be imagined." "These citizens," he averred, "rather gloried in having the world know that progress has not laid hands on that section of the country."[15] He added, however, that the inhabitants were "most obliging," and residents who recall the great event remember that the film crew were received very hospitably. Mrs. H. B. Marshall of Blue Grass clearly remembered that Barthelmess and his wife (the film actress Mary Hay) were lodged and served separately in a private home while the rest of the crew stayed at the Monterey Hotel.[16] High-spirited good fellowship, evident in several photographs taken by Mrs. Marshall and Cronjager, made for cheerful working conditions. King recalled that Blue Grass was "the only location I ever went to in my life where I never changed a thing."[17]

Although exterior shooting took place in Blue Grass and vicinity, Monterey served as the headquarters of the company. The Monterey Hotel, a pleasant rambling frame structure built in 1904, reopened to house the company; it provided a simple--although hardly primitive--homey, boardinghouse-style environment. There were communal bathrooms, high ceilings, a wide veranda with rocking chairs, and electricity until 11:00 p.m.

In Blue Grass, the company took their midday meals in the Hidy Hotel, in reality a boardinghouse. Mrs. Marshall, who worked at that time in the family store at Blue Grass, remembers the visit clearly. "We'd give the cast anything they'd want if they asked for it. I reckon we would have given them the shirt off our backs." She remembers how Forrest Robinson (Grandfather Hatburn) would wander in and out of the store to borrow items he needed; and how Gladys Hulette (Esther) borrowed an apron from her mother and a "split bonnet" (a sunbonnet stiffened with cardboard rather than starch and with ribbons to the shoulder). All of Blue Grass seemed to welcome them, and at a time when, as Mrs. Luther Simmons remembers, "a dollar was a dollar," they were glad to get a dollar a day for standing around in crowd scenes.[18] Despite the "primitiveness" Barthelmess alleges he found, Blue Grass in 1921 was considerably more populous and active than it is now. There was a jeweler, a photographer, a carding mill, a bank, a sawmill, a flour mill (in the vicinity), two doctors, and the Hidy Hotel. The Hidys also operated a movie theatre sans music on Saturdays (admission one quarter). Mrs. Hidy, who used to dress in furs and made her husband walk with a cane, fashioned the flywhisks Mrs. Kinemon used, which was a standard item in homes of the area.

The Marshalls' store was then, as it is now, a center of the community (although it is actually the Puffenbargers' store across the street that was used in the picture). "Saturday night would look like Reno, and people would come from 30 miles around," recalls Nona Wilfong. "You'd have to push your way in, and the air would be so thick with tobacco smoke you couldn't see." Hamburgers were a dime, and if you wanted crackers, you would reach into a barrel and buy a handful for a penny.[19]

The coming of the crew to Blue Grass was a memorable event--"one of the most exciting things [to happen in the area]," recalls a lady who went out daily to view the filming, joining mothers, children, babies, and those men in the condition that citizens of Blue Grass referred to as Loafers' Glory. One was struck to remember that the handsome star Richard Barthelmess looked just like he did in the picture!; but this was not the case for Ernest Torrence, remembers Mrs. Luther Simmons about the actor who played Luke Hatburn: "He was such a nice person without all that make-up on... he was a gentleman."[20]

"Scoop" Swecker, a resident of Blue Grass, was 12 years old in 1921, and he remembers a number of vivid details as he followed the crew: how the trout was already in the bucket in the trout-spearing scene; how Torrence was instructed to show his hunger by biting into an onion from the soil, and the distaste on his face when he spits out the onion off camera; how ("by gosh!") Gladys Hulette (who played Esther) was the prettiest thing he had ever seen.[21]

King told a reporter that "we must get the real atmosphere of the Virginia mountains. This is not a story of a feud or moonshiners and we have to go down among these people, absorb their mannerisms and ideas."[22] King rehearsed each actor until his role was as familiar "as an old shirt."

To prepare Torrence for his portrayal of the heavy, King suggested that Luke Hatburn is essentially "not a mean man at all"; rather he is so ignorant that he might kill a cat with a stone not out of malice but to "see the guts spill." Like his successor in Deliverance, John Boorman's similar study of ignorant depravity, Luke operates at a level barely human. One afternoon on the veranda of the Monterey Hotel, King pointed out a bedraggled man shuffling down the street, "the most dilapidated man you ever saw." King asked Torrence to study him closely; Torrence excused himself and came back in half an hour now wearing the tattered clothes of the bedraggled man. "What'd you do with the body?" King asked. Torrence explained that he caught the fellow and took him to a store where he exchanged new clothes for Luke's costume. To suggest Luke's desperate hunger, King instructed him to pull an onion out of a garden as he walks by, and sink his teeth into it[23]--the kind of improvisation which described what King means by showing rather than telling.

The picture, released in 1922, achieved instant and universal success. In its final issue for the year, Billboard rated the best pictures in this order: Orphans of the Storm, Robin Hood, The Prisoner of Zenda, The Count of Monte Cristo, Nanook of the North, Blood and Sand, Tol'able David, Smilin' Thru, and Grandma's Boy. Griffith's Orphans of the Storm was considered by Billboard to be "deservedly the best." Griffith himself, however, was delighted to see his quondam property Tol'able David brought so successfully to the screen; after its successful opening, he offered Barthelmess congratulations and rendered the opinion that it was "one of the best pictures I have ever seen." He took

Barthelmess in his arms and told him how proud he was of his former player and his new picture.[24]

The cognoscenti agreed with this judgment. Heywood Broun in the New York World commended the "remarkable feeling which [the director] has for the atmosphere."[25] From 34 film choices that year, readers of the then prestigious Photoplay voted Tol'able David the year's best picture, thereby earning for the film the coveted Gold Medal Photoplay Award.

Europe went wild over the picture, as its director later recalled.[26] The reviews from across the United States were encomiastic: "perfection," said the Baltimore Sun; "magnificent," exclaimed the San Francisco Chronicle;[27] "it is impossible to avoid superlatives," raved the St. Louis Post-Dispatch;[28] it would "go down in motion picture history as one of the greatest productions," predicted the Chicago Journal.[29] And how, one might wonder, did it play in Peoria? "It is the sort of picture," concluded a reviewer in the Peoria Transcript, "that will make you shout before you leave your seat, 'By golly, wasn't that a peach! We must bring mother to see this'--the greatest of all screen masterpieces produced up to this date."[30]

The trade press issued similarly glowing notices: The New York Exhibitors Trade Review found the picture "a sure remedy for commercial illnesses." In hailing Barthelmess' bold move into independent production, Motion Picture News observed that "evidences of broken box office records and spellbound audiences continue to point out that the star's initial venture for himself has created a veritable sensation."[31] Only Valentino among the rising actors of the new decade shone more brightly.

Barthelmess and King went on to make three additional pictures for Inspiration--The Seventh Day (1922), The Bond Boy (1922), and Fury (1923), all of which were successful except The Seventh Day ("a dog," King felt). Under the aegis of Inspiration King directed two fine Lillian Gish films, The White Sister (1923) and Romola (1924). Despite their distinguished contributions to the company, Barthelmess and King began having troubles with Duell. But when Lillian Gish discovered Duell's undoubted and shameless victimization of her trust, Inspiration was in trouble.

The incredible story recounted in Gish's The Movies, Mr. Griffith, and Me indicates that Duell wanted not only to control Gish but to marry her. Finding himself flatly turned down, he sued her for breach of contract. Gish's defense against these unconscionable pressures resulted in Duell's total disgrace, his disbarment, and his being heavily fined for perjury.[32]

When Inspiration expired, Barthelmess had made for the company a total of 18 films, and now his career had begun to sag. But when he signed on at First National, his fortunes revived with The Patent Leather Kid (1927), a role that won him a nomination in the first Academy Awards competition. Now in his thirties, he was no longer easily cast in youthful roles; and, additionally, when sound required that the gods speak, Barthelmess' nasal baritone was not quite what one might have fantasized. He was still an important name but less and less of a draw despite some excellent roles, e.g., the courageous flyer in Hawks' Dawn Patrol (1930). For his last memorable picture, Howard Hawks' Only Angels Have Wings (1939), he returned, curiously enough, to the kind of role which won his fame in Tol'able David. Once again he played the reputed coward whose mettle is triumphantly tested by an arduous journey. He made no further pictures after 1943. After the war, he retired to Long Island, where he lived until his death by cancer in 1963. He left an estate of more than a million dollars.

The debonair Virginian Warner Richmond (who played the sympathetic Allen) continued to play prominent second leads (and occasionally first) through the decade, although again Tol'able David was his best picture. Richmond's career had declined notably by the end of the 1930s, when he was reduced to making cowboy films for Monogram. In 1939 he fell from a horse, and in one of those uncanny turns of fate which the accident in Tol'able David seems proleptically to have envisioned, he remained paralyzed for the rest of his life, ending his days in the Motion Picture Actors' Retirement Home in 1948.

Gladys Hulette of the silken tresses and compassionate eyes defied the vogue for flappers and stayed busy as an artless innocent until the coming of sound, when the calls stopped for her as they did for many more celebrated actors. Miss Hulette has lived recently as a ward of the state in a place eerily called the Monterey Sanitarium in Rosemead, California. When she was last interviewed by the author in 1981, her spirits, however, seemed cheerful; her eyes were still ethereally blue and her complexion of such a coloring that one can believe Scoop Swecker's recollection of her in Blue Grass that she was the prettiest thing he had ever seen.

As long as people study the art of the motion picture, Greenstream will still shine, and David and Esther will forever be young in the land of streams in an American version of Arcadia. And there, too, is the presence of mortality, as Guercino's picture must remind us and to which the fate of the rest of the actors whose bright image the celluloid has captured will testify. Against that inevitability art is our sole protest.

NOTES

1. In 1921, however, this hamlet was called Crabbottom.

2. Mr. and Mrs. Kenton Rexrode. Interview with the author, November 23, 1979.

3. Henry King. Interview with the author, August 8, 1980. Most viewers today find it difficult to accept Mrs. Kinemon's dragging herself through the mud to keep her boy from going after the Hatburns. David's conflict of values--the dilemma of values which defines what moral problems are all about--opposes the conflicting claims of David's duty to his family as a son and to himself as a young man. When questioned by the author as to whether the business of Mrs. Kinemon's tackling her son to keep him home might not be excessive, King replied with this story:

> When my father had died, I was about 12--he had died three or four months before this. There was a man living near Ellison, Virginia, who had some sheep. Two dogs had killed some of his sheep, and someone identified one of those dogs as Widow King's. The other one was Dr. Oliver's--Dr. Oliver was a doctor in Ellison. The law in Virginia is that if a dog kills a sheep you have to kill it. This man went to Dr. Oliver who married later in life, and he had a baby about three. It was not unusual to see the child riding the dog or lying down on the ground with his arms around him.... He said, "Well the dog is out there with my baby in the backyard. John, if you kill that dog, I'm going to kill you." The man thought about it. Nothing more was said.
>
> He turned and walked out the door and he came to our house and he told my mother what he was after.... This dog--I shared everything I had with him, any food--he was as close to me--a boy and his dog! I went upstairs and leaned out the window and heard all that was said. My mother surrendered. So he got off his horse and tied a rope around my dog and started away. I ran to my father's trunk and got his revolver. My mother saw what I was doing. She took after me and ran across the meadow. She made one last lunge and grabbed me by the feet and I fell on my face. She held my feet.

And so, King concluded, the man escaped while the would-be young assassin was restrained only by the desperate intervention of his mother; some 20 years later that struggle was reenacted as Mrs. Kinemon desperately holds back her son from taking on the family adversary.

4. Ibid. King thought the dashing figure of the mail carrier in those days comparable to the jet pilot's image today.

5. Charles Reich, The Greening of America (Random House: New York, 1970), p. 22.

6. Pudovkin defined color "as the scarcely communicable ability to saturate the film with numerous fine and correctly observed details." (Film Technique and Film Acting, tr. and ed. Ivor Montague. Memorial edition. [Grove Press: New York, 1949; reprinted 1970], p. 124.

7. King interview, August 1981.

8. Lillian Gish with Ann Pinchot, The Movies, Mr. Griffith, and Me (Prentice-Hall: Englewood Cliffs, N.J., 1969), p. 20.

9. King interview, November 1979.

10. Ibid.

11. Ibid. King had originally tried to engage David Torrence, Ernest's brother; but King was alert to the dramatic possibilities of the tall, intense Scotsman whose success on the stage at the time was bringing him $450 per week, as King remembered.

12. A clipping (Mrs. Carolyn Harris, "My Own Richard Barthelmess," Film Play Journal [November 1921]) in Richard Barthelmess' scrapbooks on Tol'able David, Vol. II (Motion Picture Academy of Arts and Sciences Library, Hollywood, California), p. 10. Most clippings are undated. Hereafter referred to as Scrapbook.

13. King interview, August 1981.

14. Scrapbook, II, p. 29.

15. Ibid.

16. Mrs. H. B. Marshall. Interview with the author, October 18, 1980.

17. King interview, August 1981.

18. Mrs. Luther Simmons. Interview with the author, October 18, 1980.

19. Miss Nona Wilfong. Interview with the author, October 18, 1980.

20. Simmons interview, October 1980.

21. Mr. "Scoop" Swecker. Interview with the author, October 18, 1980.

22. Barthelmess quoting King. Scrapbook, II. p. 29.

23. King interview, August 1981.

24. Scrapbook, I, p. 80.

25. Scrapbook, II, p. 61.

26. King interview, August 1981.

27. Scrapbook, I, p. 2.

28. Scrapbook, II, p. 63.

29. Scrapbook, II, p. 61.

30. Scrapbook, I, p. 49.

31. Scrapbook, I, p. 3.
32. Gish, pp. 265-270.

The bedizened Belle Bennett as Stella. Laurel (Lois Moran, third from left) is aghast while her smart young friends are amused.

Chapter 4
Stella Dallas: Dreaming of Utopia

After working with his editor Stuart Heisler all day Saturday and Saturday night, King completed final cutting on his first picture for Samuel Goldwyn. Although he still retained a partnership interest in Inspiration, Goldwyn had offered him half interest in his new production in exchange for directorial services. King drove to the studio the next day and arrived about the time Goldwyn emerged from the screening room. He saw Goldwyn and two assistants walking as if they were going to a funeral.

"Good morning," King said. "You finished sooner than I thought you would."

Goldwyn looked down and muttered, "Henry, you've ruined me."

King was amazed--had he created a flop? "What are you talking about, I've 'ruined you'?"

Goldwyn grabbed him by his shoulders, then put his arm around him and said, "No one can stand it. Look at those women--they can't stand it! I've never seen anything so...." Then weeping openly, he added, "It's great! It's wonderful! It's terrific! I've never seen such a picture that can hold an audience.... Frances Marion almost passed out! It just ruined me!"[1]

Now Goldwyn's famous speech forms owed their uniqueness in part to his custom of translating idioms from Polish into English. In this instance, Goldwyn's "ruin" was an attempt to translate his sense of an emotionally devastating experience. Far from ruining Goldwyn, it gave him a box-office triumph, his biggest critical success to date, and new honors for all associated with the picture.

To examine the story from the perspective of the mid-1980s requires a suspension of disbelief in social assumptions underlying the plot of Olive Higgins Prouty's best-selling novel. Those accustomed to watching TV serials will find these assumptions more credible; indeed, in the 1930s and 40s Stella Dallas was to become one of the most popular radio soaps, on the air from 1937 to 1955.[2] Before its translation to the screen, Stella Dallas was a lavishly-budgeted stage success for Mrs. Leslie Carter in 1924.[3] The sympathetic spectator, now as then, must be able to accept conventions of sacrifice standard in such generic fare. Who today could believe the Madame X plot of sacrificial mother love? Yet the fact that it was filmed six times between 1909 and 1966 argues that mass audiences for the greater part of the century have eagerly accepted such fare. The American Film Institute Catalog (Feature Films 1921-30) lists 173 titles dealing with mothers.[4]

Sacrifice is the measure of love, and is the most graphically effective means available to the dramatist of showing its power. Silent pictures (as well as Renaissance drama, with which early film conventions curiously have much in common) again and again turn on sacrificial action. In 1921--the same year that Fox brought in one of its biggest hits in a motion picture entitled Over the Hill starring Mary Carr--King had made two pictures dealing with mother love. Salvage, a lost Pauline Frederick vehicle, carried this description in the Motion Picture News for May 28, 1921: "a tale of mother love which relies upon a spirit of self-sacrifice for its appeal, with plenty of recourse to melodramatic trimmings which appear unduly far-fetched to seem genuine." But no reviewer was to doubt the genuineness of his next picture, Tol'able David. King drew upon personal experience to dramatize how David's love for his mother restrains him from seeking requital from the Hatburns, and Mrs. Kinemon, it is clear, holds the family together. For King this primal bond connected him with the theme in the most personal way, for his mother was the central figure in his life. King's widow, Ida Davis King, has observed the recurring presence of the maternal theme in her husband's films. And, quite significantly, at the age of 96 King died invoking his mother's name, Martha Ellen.

The altruism of sacrifice figures notably in such King vehicles as The Bond Boy (1922), Merely Mary Ann (1931), and The Woman in Room 13 (1932); and King's favorite picture, he once averred, was the charmingly tender adaptation of O. Henry's "The Gift of the Magi," in which a young couple mutually sacrifice their favorite possessions to obtain Christmas gifts for each other. When the motif of sacrifice is added with mother love, the two unquestionably popular themes gain added power, as in Stella Dallas. In 1931, King remade Over the Hill, which, although now forgotten, still is powerful in its dramatization of a mother's sacrifices for children and husband; in that picture the protagonist (Mae Marsh) is in two scenes iconically identified with the most familiar American painting of the time, Whistler's Mother. Religious imagery, in which the Madonna motif is prominent, may be observed in such films as Ramona (1935) and The Bravados (1959). The Song of Bernadette (1943) is, moveover, a celebration of the Divine Mother. One can see then why Prouty's tale of sacrificing mother love should prove a congenial subject for King.

All works of art are necessarily of their age, partaking, in Hamlet's phrase, of the form and pressure of the time. As times change, so the conventions of a story may date, as the "bed-trick" and the many testing devices of faithful wives, so prominent in the drama of the Elizabethans, seem preposterous today. Truth-to-life, which is the greatest revelation art can offer, may result from the use of the very conventions quite unacceptable today. Stella's sacrifice may seem incredible, but given the conventions of social demarcation barring her acceptance--conventions still apparent, although somewhat different in American life 60 years later--Stella Dallas is not as dated as it might first appear.

In assessing the work of the outstanding American directors in 1933, the late Dwight Macdonald considered Tol'able David "one of the most perfect movies ever made," but Stella Dallas the more remarkable film, remarkable because it was "the epic of the externally undramatic middle classes." He went on to describe the film as "not shrilly sensational melodrama" but "a deeply felt drama of a middle-class mother and her middle-class daughter." Deeply felt, certainly, but Stella is not, as Macdonald thought, "just a bit 'common' according to bourgeois standards."[5] She comes from the proletariat, having been favored by chance in the accident of her marriage to Stephen Grosvenor. In a home where her father (who picks his feet) is too lazy to remove boiling coffee from the stove, Stella, slavey to her callous family, entertains sentimental dreams of romance. Trapped in the milltown of Millhampton, she watches from her porch (hung with washing) files of workers going back and forth from their factory housing to their mechanical jobs. Her father in undershirt and suspenders kicks his son who hits his younger brother: a bit of business revealing the endless cycle of casual violence in that environment. In some magazine she picks out (with a hairpin) an ad showing how morning-glory vines can transform a house into a "love nest." The vines she plants flourish, becoming, in the words of the title, "a clever little trap" which will catch the man who is to rescue her from Millhampton, where, as the title has it, "the wheels of life grind relentlessly on."

Macdonald thought that the catastrophe of the film "is precipitated by nothing more sensational than the bourgeois idea of some people being 'nice' and others being 'common'."[6] He was right, except that "nothing more" is too reductive, even trivializing, as a description of Stella's real social problem. Stella wants to escape the squalor surrounding her; she is sensitive enough to want the finer things, but not educated enough to free herself from her conditioning. She is fatally destined to remain in her class regardless of heroic attempts to break with the past and to be accepted by the strata above her.

Heroic is the term to describe those efforts, for if Stella Dallas is the epic of the middle-class, the eponymous protagonist defines the values of the group by the very fact that she cannot belong, and will never be able to, but to that end she sacrifices her life and happiness. Status in the American haute-bourgeoisie must ineluctably elude her, but not her daughter Laurel, whose passage into the world of money and manners is assured once Stella removes herself. But in another sense Laurel is unwittingly the sacrifice offered on the altar of the middle-class. The complex of values, the belief system of that class so dramatically defined by the picture, is, practically speaking, a cult of which Stephen's true love Helen Morrison (Alice Joyce) is the high priestess. Her social stratum, which is to say that of the upper middle-class depicted in novel and film, is a closed society; but the gates to this privileged world swing open to the aspirant who masters, as Stella never can, the social shibboleths.

Appropriate artifacts also help to define membership. Mrs. Morrison's membership is signified by her home in the city and her home in the country. She keeps horses for herself and her sons to ride in Central Park. Her sons, in contrast to Stella's ragged brothers, dress for dinner (black-tie) and gather around the Atwater-Kent in the living room, where French windows open upon a landscaped garden. She keeps a butler, and bowls of cut flowers are placed in the guest room. Laurel's spacious quarters feature a chaise longue, a canopied bed, and a bookcase which appears to contain Dr. Eliot's Five-Foot Shelf (works chosen by Dr. Charles Eliot of Harvard for anyone desiring to spend "15 minutes a day" in the pursuit of education).

But if there is one symbol which signifies visually Stella's social ignorance, it is clothes. Goldwyn's talented _costumier_ Sophie Wachner picked up Prouty's description of Stella's dress (King had marked this description in his copy of the novel), and the contrast with Helen Morrison's attire tells it all. Mrs. Morrison's riding habit is carefully tailored. The straight lines of her loose-hanging chiffon (a day-dress for the home) is exquisitely telling in contrast to Stella's grotesquely fussy ruffles and feathers. Nineteen twenty-five was the year in which Chanel revolutionized American fashion; that was the year Gloria Swanson, who had spent months in Paris making _Madame Sans-Gêne_, helped to introduce these elegantly simple fashions to the United States. But it was not just a matter of getting outfitted by Chanel. Poor Stella lacked the other _sine qua non_ of acceptance: manners.

There are arcane codes in the social world of dinners and country club events to which Stella--strong but wrong--aspires. Early after her marriage Stella is seen curling her hair while she reads an etiquette book that is 20 years out-of-date. She extends her little finger with exaggerated refinement and offers her hand with regal grandeur when parting from the headmistress of Laurel's school. At a time when socially prominent women "painted" very sparingly, heavy mascara and lipstick--which Stephen vainly implores her to remove--define Stella's eyes and lips. At the country club where she is "a noticeable figure," she soaks her teacakes and leaves a spoon in her cup. Smartly dressed women make incredulous eyes at each other when Stella effusively greets the buffoonish riding-master Ed Munn, whose brilliantined hair, sleeve garters, striped shirt and floral tie signal a similar social unacceptability. Ed's coarse parlor tricks--pretending to swallow a knife at the tea-table--shock the elegant ladies at the club, as does the familiarity of his greeting when he kisses the palm of Stella's hand.

For Stella, Ed's bawdy humor and vitality (he runs up stairs which others climb) answer a need unprovided by the decorous Stephen. Stephen refuses to shake the hand of the riding-master whom Stella has impulsively invited home. As the titles read, "The weight of her lay heavily upon [Stephen's] heart." And no wonder. Stella, a slatternly housekeeper, employs as charwoman and babysitter a pipe-smoking hulk of a woman who sleeps on the job. The apartment, with its player piano, scraps of material scattered on the floor, gingerbread ornamentation, and fussy curtains, tell us what we need to know about Stella's tastes. When Stephen leaves Stella and Millhampton to pursue his career in New York, those tastes have now no circumscription, and Stella continues seeing Munn, much to Laurel's disgust.

Stella does know enough to offer Laurel the advantages: these mean sending her to Miss Philliburn's Select School for Girls and vacationing in summer resorts where she can meet on wide verandahs with wicker chairs, "nice young people." Stella, who cannot swim, golf, or play tennis, has made sure that Laurel is an adept at such pursuits. Whereas other visitors (improbably) read Shaw's Man and Superman and Ouspensky's Tertium Organum, Stella prefers the latest Elinor Glyn and Breezy Tales.

Two key episodes illustrate how Stella's presence is a threat to Laurel's passage into the privileged world. For Laurel's tenth birthday Stella has prepared an elaborate party. In an establishing shot, the viewer sees the apartment festooned with decorations: expensive favors decorate the table upon which is set a huge cake, flowers are in profusion, and two maids in starched uniforms stand ready in the kitchen. Laurel practices her greetings while her mother beams approval, and the two wait in joyous anticipation. But by the announced time, no one has come; a half hour passes and daughter and mother are still waiting. Steps are heard in the hallway--but these belong to visitors going elsewhere. Then a messenger arrives bearing a letter of doom to Stella, informing her of Laurel's "discontinuance" from Miss Philliburn's; for Miss Philliburn has learned of Stella's indiscreet behavior with the flashy Munn. The implication is clear: Laurel and her mother are thereby both ostracized from society. Stella puts on a brave front: the two decide to have their own party. Calmly, King's meditative medium shot surveys the scene. They are separated at each end of the table by the enormous cake; then the two pull their chairs closer together. But the party favors do not pop. A two-shot shows mother and daughter staring into space as they try hard to eat their ice cream, swallowing with difficulty, restraining the brimming tears. The scene perfectly summarizes the nobility of Stella's intentions and her inability to execute them.

Stella's scheme for Laurel to be with her own kind pays off, however, when she takes Laurel to an expensive lakeside resort for several weeks. On her own, Laurel immediately finds her place among the trim, cloche-hatted young women and handsome young men in white flannels and striped jackets. All goes joyously for Laurel as long as her mother is confined to her bed; but on the very day that Laurel is courted by the dashing Richard Grosvenor (played with sensitivity by the youthful Douglas Fairbanks, Jr.), Stella emerges from her seclusion. While Laurel and her friends are meeting their friends at the lakeside, Stella, bedizened with filbert-sized pearls, carrying a ruffled parasol and wearing a gown of zebra stripes with furbelows, marches inexorably forward, signalling to Laurel the approach of disaster. If she acknowledges her mother, she will lose her friends. Hastily she pretends to lose her watch, and she and Richard hurry away in a canoe. Social suicide seems inevitable if her friends meet her mother. That very evening Laurel packs their trunks to board the Pullman which will remove them as quickly as possible from the scene of further embarrassment.

Ensconced in their upper and lower berths, while each thinks the other asleep, Laurel and Stella overhear a party of young vacationers waiting for their berths to be made: they are discussing "that dreadful creature" who is Laurel's mother. Stella now realizes, despite all her will and effort, that she will forever be an impediment in the path of Laurel's advancement.

That is the realization which is to bring her later to the home of Mrs. Morrison, whom Stephen would marry were he free of Stella. For this occasion Stella wears an embroidered satin jacket with a shawl collar over a lacy jabot. Her ring-encrusted hands clutch a beaded purse; atop her peroxided curls is a hat extravagantly feathered with osprey plumes. Helen Morrison, her dark hair caught in a low chignon at the back of her neck, wears a simple white diaphonous chiffon. She wears no jewelry, neither on this occasion nor on any other. In a two-shot the women are seen surmounting these formidable barriers of clothes and class to recognize a maternal bond. Stella proposes to grant Stephen his divorce in order that Laurel will have a proper home--that way "the wedding invitations will read right." Stella lovingly examines Laurel's room, patting a cushion, testing the mattress, and taking a single rose "to remember the room by."

But as Laurel knows that she, herself, is the center of her mother's life, that sacrifice is not one Laurel will accept. The result is that both women are now miserable, for Laurel is without friends or future and Stella is incapable of bringing her either: "Stella's heart cried out with pain. 'What can I do now to save her?'" In a beautifully paced scene, Stella, in despair, goes to the bathroom, looks out the window, stares at a gas fixture, reaches for the gascock to turn it on, then, recoiling in horror, turns it off, and screams at what she has done. It is then she espies Ed Munn's card: one way remains to drive Laurel to her father, for if Stella will marry Munn (at this point a drunken derelict) Laurel will be sure to leave home. That sacrifice, utterly ruinous to Stella, will secure Laurel's future happiness.

The final scene, perhaps the most familiar in the film, literally frames that happiness for Stella, while simultaneously distancing her so that she will never be part of it. On a wet night in Manhatten, Stella, now looking old and fearful, gazes at an upstairs window where Laurel stands among the lights and flowers radiant in her lacy bridal gown. Through a window she can see the bride come forward to join Richard Grosvenor. The feathers on her hat wet and bedraggled, Stella nonetheless fills her eyes with this moment of glory. A policeman moves her on, but now the rain has stopped. Behind her streams the light of hope from the bridal window. Stella Redemptrix, the Mater Dolorosa, passes on. The oldest story, King once said, was that of the man who dies to save others; Stella Dallas is another version of that story.

In real life such sacrifice would be exemplary if there were a golden world peopled by young princes as handsome as Fairbanks and by ladies as lovely and serenely graceful as Alice Joyce. Film and fiction ignored for a long time the psychic cost of acquiring wealth, or of even earning a living. Money seems unworthy of attention, for in the celluloid social world do not secretaries and shop girls live in spacious flats? and are not furs and limousines accessible to pretty girls who know how to dress so as to catch the eye of the boss or a playboy millionaire? In the films of the 1920s, such situations were familiar in the work of Gloria Swanson and Clara Bow. Moviegoers, eager to escape the dailyness of desolate towns and tenements, did not want to be reminded that Cinderella is a fairy tale. The life of the rich, so attractively presented by Mrs. Morrison, is in Utopia--which is to say literally nowhere.

Goldwyn's desire to make a successful film began with buying the rights to Stella Dallas and then, as was his custom, with assembling the best talent available. Frances Marion, perhaps the most gifted scenarist of the 1920s, reported that everyone was surprised at Goldwyn's purchase of Prouty's novel. By 1925 "his pictures were becoming the sterling on silver," and he spared no expense to get the best. The public seemed to be clamoring for melodrama or spectaculars, so it was unusual for a master showman to choose so simple a tale.[7] In addition to Frances Marion, the film brought together Arthur Edeson, whose crisp photography had served Douglas Fairbanks, Sr., so well in such fare as Robin Hood (1922) and The Thief of Bagdad (1924), and Stuart Heisler, who after five years of learning his trade as a

Stella (Belle Bennett) watches the marriage of her daughter Laurel (Lois Morgan) to Richard Grosvenor (Douglas Fairbanks, Jr.) while his mother (Beatrix Pryor) looks on. Note the reflection of Stella's face in the lower right-hand corner of the window.

cutter, had just completed a highly-commended piece of editing for Goldwyn in George Fitzmaurice's The Dark Angel (1925). King, noted for this collaborative ability, respected Heisler's judgment and apparently deferred to him on more than one occasion. As Heisler remembered:

> I put it the way I thought it should be, and I'd show it to him. If I'm a film editor, the word "editor" means you've got some power to do something about it.... You have to tell the story as simply as you possibly can, and you can't complicate it.

Heisler recalled that King shot a lot of angles (which is surprisingly uncharacteristic of King's work): "I had more damn choices of what to use!" Heisler said that Goldwyn thought that "many different angles would make it look like a bigger picture." When the picture was first assembled, it was 16,000 or 17,000 feet long. Heisler reported the astonishing information (not verifiable elsewhere) that to eliminate 5,000 or 6,000 feet they cut out a character who was played by Henry King![8] This seems questionable, for there is no male character in the novel who is not featured in the picture, and by all reports King had last acted in 1920. King did remember that he had inserted, at Goldwyn's insistence, a delirium tremens scene with Ed Munn, which so disturbed the sneak preview audience that it unbalanced the film, and Goldwyn withdrew it immediately.

King's work, however, is not prolix in Stella Dallas, and none of King's work better testifies to his ability to convey much information in a few images than the opening sequence of Stella's life in Millhampton. With his customary care for authenticity he photographed a row of houses near a factory (the locale is not known) and then reproduced the sad little cottage that was to constitute Stella's "sordid surroundings." Sordid it is: Stella's father is an unkempt lout who treats his daughter like a mindless servant. He warms his feet in the oven with the bread. Her brothers are wild children who mock her attempts at romance. (In what must be the first "moon shot," one boy mischievously exposes himself when the shade collapses in a window behind the courting couple.) They live on a street where men walk listlessly to work at machines that grind out lives like the mills of the gods. Despite the fact that Stella cannot belong to the class above her, a wistful prettiness sets her apart from this mean environment. She plants vines of morning glories all over the porch in an attempt to touch the setting with poetry--and to catch the lonely young lawyer who passes the cottage daily. Thus early in the picture Stella is sympathetically established against the drab milieu, while simultaneously the manipulativeness of her plan to turn her home into a "love nest" will make her an unsuitable mate for Stephen Dallas.

But King's success owes as much to the actors as to any aspect of the production. In one of the great performances in screen history--magnificent is not too extravagant an adjective--Belle Bennett registers a remarkable emotional range: folly, agony, joy, grief, while simultaneously evoking in the viewer profound sympathy and painful embarrassment. One scene, for which credit is probably due to King, deserves comment. After Laurel speeds away on the train that is to take her to her new life, Stella's face is a study in grief. In the ladies' room at the depot, she keeps trying vainly to re-apply her mascara. As the tears course freely down her cheeks streaking her make-up, the Mater Dolorosa is transformed into the persona of the sad clown, and her face registers the keenest pathos. A hard-faced woman reaches out and offers a cigarette. "Don't worry, dearie," she comforts, "it all comes out in the wash."

Never was a choice so felicitous as the selection of Belle Bennett for the title role. Lois Moran recalls that Bennett wanted the role so badly that she began to overeat to make herself look more matronly.[9] Perhaps the fact that Bennett had lost her 17-year-old son just the month before shooting began deepened the pathos of her performance; certainly Moran and Fairbanks, who were both 16 at the time, found her remarkably warm and kind. Her eyes, recollects Moran, were especially effective indicators as to how she was feeling.

An all-round thespian, Belle Bennett was born to a theatrical company and had since childhood played in tents and touring companies. King had known Bennett when he had played opposite her at the Balboa Film Company about 1915-16. She had made two or three pictures that were not especially successful, but in 1921 King had seen her opposite Tyrone Power, Sr., in The Wandering Jew, a role which won her great applause. King thought her performance "just tremendous."[10] At that age of 34, when she was chosen to play Stella, she reached the peak of her career, but whether from lack of will or from the absence of good direction, she never equalled herself again. In 1927 she had the title role in a picture called Mother, and in 1928, she scored notable success in John Ford's Mother Machree. She died in 1932 at the age of 41.

It was Goldwyn, however, who deserves the credit for having found Lois Moran. Lois had been taken to Paris by a mother eager to give her talented daughter every advantage. While dancing in the Paris National Opera, she was discovered by the avant-garde filmmaker Marcel L'Herbier who featured her in two films. When Lois heard that Goldwyn was casting for Romeo and Juliet, she thought herself at 14 fully capable of the role and sent Goldwyn her picture with an accompanying note. By the time

Goldwyn interviewed her in Paris, Shakespeare was out and Prouty was in. A voracious reader, she had just finished Stella Dallas and knew Laurel's situation; Goldwyn was impressed and immediately tested her for the part. When she came to the States to take a role in Marc Connelly's The Wisdom Tooth, King went down to Atlantic City where the show was trying out. As Goldwyn's test was "just a big close-up," King wanted to see if she was as good as Goldwyn thought. King recollected:

> She was 15--and looked 15--but when Sam told us that she was a dancer, I was concerned that she would have big muscular calves, and we needed someone with slender, young-looking legs. Sam said, "I don't know what her legs look like. I don't look at children's legs." When they arrived back in the States, I went all the way to Atlantic City to meet Mrs. Moran, Lois, and Sam for dinner. I said, "Lois, the reason I'm down here is to see your legs." She put her legs out and said, "How are they?" I said, "That one's good, they're fine, you're in."
>
> One day Sam said to me, "What are you going to do about Lois when she's supposed to be 11? How are you going to make a 15-year-old look like 11?" I sent over to a school, got four or five 11-year-olds, and had Sophie Wachner, who was doing wardrobe, costume them for a test. We had Lois put on rib stockings to shape her legs like a child's and dressed her like the rest of the girls. I put all six of them together and panned the camera across them back and forth. When Sam saw the test he became terribly confused and final ly said, "Henry, are you pulling my leg? Is that or isn't that Lois Moran? I never would have believed it. She looks more like 11 years old than any of the 11-year-olds!"[11]

Goldwyn wanted to sign her for a seven-year contract, but her mother thought seven years a long time. She signed instead for one picture--at $200 per week, exactly what she was being paid on the stage.[12] None of her later roles in film attracted much attention in a series of undistinguished films, although she did receive acclaim when she played on Broadway in the famous Gershwin hit of 1931, Of Thee I Sing, after which she gave up her career to marry the aviation pioneer Clarence Young. For the rest of their lives she maintained her friendship with Hersholt, King, and Ronald Colman who was, she said, "my idol."

Among the many stars King discovered or fashioned, none shines more brightly than Colman, an actor who invariably combined taste and distinction with a sensitive but masculine screen presence. King had chosen an old play called The White Sister (1923) as Lillian Gish's first vehicle for Inspiration Pictures. The picture, planned as the largest Hollywood production to be filmed abroad, lacked a suitable leading man for the role of the military officer and scientist. One night at the Empire Theatre in New York, King's first wife, Gypsy, noticed a good-looking man (Ronald Colman) in a small part in a play called La Tendresse. She turned to her husband and said, "That's the man you're looking for; that's Giovanni Severini."

At an interview the next day Colman was diffident: "Mr. King, I'd just like to tell you something before you go any further. In London they tested me. Everyone said I didn't photograph well and wouldn't go over in pictures. I've been in pretty rough straits over here. Mr. Miller [Henry Miller, producer] put me in a show, and I think I'd better stay where I know what I'm doing." King asked him if he would make a test. Colman replied that he would like to, but that everything had gone against him. As King reported, Colman seemed to be stiff and somewhat ill at ease:

> In making the test I wanted to break down any barriers. So I sat and asked him embarrassing questions to take his mind off the camera. At least I broke down that stiffness he had. Between takes in the test, I got rid of his pompadoured hairdo and put a moustache on him. By the time we got through with all of this we were well-enough acquainted and I said, "Mr. Colman, you're 90 percent in. I can't make a final decision until I see the film, but I think you're the man I'm looking for." He said, "I can't believe it. When you see the film you're going to give up and say forget it."
>
> Since Lillian Gish was going to play in this, I wanted to have her see what she thought of the test. It was exactly as I thought. You could see the development straight through to the mustache--it made him into Giovanni. Lillian said, "The only thing is he is an English actor, and they're awfully stiff."
>
> "I don't think he will be."
>
> "Well, Henry, it's up to you. You're the one that has to make the picture."
>
> I signed Colman to go to Italy, paid all expenses and gave him $450 a week. And there was never a man so surprised as he. Ten days later we were on the boat Providence headed for Italy.[13]

Colman became one of the most distinguished and durable leading men in screen history. King directed him twice more for Goldwyn; once in the great Western spectacular The Winning of

Barbara Worth (1926) and again in a circus story, The Magic Flame (1927). He and Banky, starring in both, became one of the silents' most romantic couples.

Few screen actors can owe more to a director than Jean Hersholt owed to Henry King. Although he was well-established by 1925, having played in a number of notable pictures since 1915, his superb performance in Greed, Stroheim's masterpiece of 1924, must have been weighty in his selection as the practical-joking riding-master Ed Munn, whose manners become progressively more offensive. He scratches his armpit, makes bad jokes, chug-a-lugs his beer, pokes his finger into Laurel's mouth, and shoots beebees at fellow passengers on a train. But beneath the crass exterior Hersholt invests the character with animal high-spirits which are the source of Stella's attraction to him. There is an uneasy moment when he earns some sympathy as Stephen rejects his extended hand. Munn is crestfallen, but then he puts on a genial face and exits with the line: "Well, as the roof said to the cyclone, I'll be off now." That the actor playing this buffoon should in time also come to play the sensitive Dr. Christian is a tribute to Hersholt's extraordinary versatility.

The coming of sound, however, dealt a blow to Hersholt's career. King rescued him from neglect for his early sound picture Hell Harbor (1930) in which his Danish accent was acceptable for a character part. (In this picture he was cast once again as the antagonist opposite Gibson Gowland, his co-star of Greed.) But as King related, "Hollywood soon ran out of parts of him," and again his career languished. When King in 1936 was preparing the remarkable picture developed around Dr. Allan Dafoe, the doctor to the Dionne quintuplets, King once again nominated Hersholt for the title role. Zanuck demurred: "Oh, hell, he has an accent broad enough to cut with a knife." But King pointed out that Canada drew people from all over the earth, and some didn't even speak English: "Perhaps," he argued, "it would be unusual to have this man without an accent."[14] Fox picked up his contract from MGM and starred him in the role which would forever after identify him with the benevolent sage. King was to select him again as the slum priest in Seventh Heaven (1937) and as the serious musician in Alexander's Ragtime Band (1938). In 1939 Hersholt became Dr. Christian for the remainder of his career, and was forever associated in the public mind with that humanitarian figure of radio, film, and television. He died in 1956, mourned widely by the public and the industry.

For good reason Alice Joyce, whom Lois Moran remembers as a serene and warm presence, earned the soubriquet "Madonna of the Screen." Her large liquescent eyes that gaze upon Stella with sympathy and understanding communicate spiritual depths. A Vitagraph star who moved in the 1920s from ingénues to older roles, Joyce was also cast as Clara Bow's mother in the Paramount hit Dancing Mothers (1926), was featured in the first Beau Geste of that same year, and played opposite George Arliss in the early talkie The Green Goddess (1930), having also starred in the earlier version of that picture in 1921. Her screen persona combined a touch of exoticism with grace and elegance.

Despite attempts to exploit the numinousness of his name, Douglas Fairbanks, Jr.'s, first picture was not especially successful and the two which followed were routine. It took Stella Dallas to reveal his innate charm, good manners, and sensitivity. A memorable scene (especially appreciated by the Times reviewer) occurs when Richard kisses Laurel. King refused--against Goldwyn's and Frances Marion's advice--to allow his young actor to take Moran into his arms for a big kiss; instead Richard delicately kisses Laurel on the check--in King's words "like nice boys and girls do it."[15] King introduced a delicate piece of business when he asked Fairbanks, in order to signal the passage of months when he sees Laurel the second time, to smooth a fledgling mustache. In time Fairbanks achieved stardom, but he has become better known as a leading international social figure. He was decorated in 1949 by George VI.

Goldwyn premiered Stella Dallas for a film and theatrical audience at the Apollo Theatre on November 16, 1925, an event honoring Ethel Barrymore, then the leading actress of the American stage. While critical responses on such occasions must be discounted because of the customary indiscriminate heaping of superlatives, there was this evening an extraordinary enthusiasm. Miss Barrymore had averred in the program that it was "the best motion picture I have ever seen," and that she had never cried so in a motion picture, and rarely so in a theatre.[16] Bursts of applause constantly interrupted the picture, and the acclaim at the end made it, in the words of one journalist, "One of the finest openings New York has ever seen."[17] Goldwyn wired King it was "the greatest reception a motion picture ever received." Frederick James Smith, critic on the New York World, considered it "one of the greatest pictures of the screen." Danny Dannenburg, owner and editor of Film Daily, telegraphed King the news that the picture had "rocked New York['s] theatrical world." James R. Quirk, the owner and editor of Photoplay, the most prestigious organ of film journalism, wired that he was "reluctant to use superlatives but this is one of the few really great motion pictures ever made." Olive Higgins Prouty sent her gratitude and congratulated King on his "wonderful generalship" in directing the character. Barthelmess acknowledged that the picture was "all the critics say." "No director," he noted "can get more from his people than yourself [referring to King]." That tribute was enthusiastically endorsed by Belle Bennett who was now radiating in the splendid success the picture was enjoying. She thanked King for his faith in her, and for "tender, kind and perfect direction during the months when Stella and I needed gentle intelligent words whispered." It was a "perfect understanding." "All my life," she went on, "you shall be the great King of directors and I your faithful subject."

Stella Dallas marked the high point of his association with Goldwyn. Just as he followed Tol'able David with the deplorable The Seventh Day, so King now listlessly directed for Goldwyn a Potash and Perlmutter comedy, Partners Again--"one of the worst pictures" in the words of his editor Stuart Heisler. Still to come were the two Colman-Banky vehicles, one of which (Barbara Worth) introduced a lanky cowboy named Gary Cooper. King did not plumb the emotional depths of Stella Dallas until 1930, when he again told the story of sacrificing mother love in the minor masterpiece, Over the Hill.

Goldwyn retained a strong regard for King's work and asked him to retell Stella Dallas in sound, but King wasn't interested in remaking his own work: he had similarly refused Harry Cohn at Columbia who had asked him to do Tol'able David as a talkie. King signed over gratis his half-ownership in Stella Dallas to Goldwyn (for which Goldwyn anonymously sent him a diamond-studded wrist watch).[18] Goldwyn then asked King Vidor to direct the version which most people know starring Barbara Stanwyck with Anne Shirley (1937), also a financial spectacular. But King Vidor's set-ups are Henry King's, and the latter film is as much a re-creation of the original as Henry King's version of Seventh Heaven that same year is a re-creation of Borzage's classic of 1927. And although Stanwyck is creditable as Stella, she is no Belle Bennett, anymore than Simone Simon is Janet Gaynor. The remake is nevertheless a strong story, its confrontation of the social problems of the middle class still valid in 1938. They are not without pertinence in addressing the increasingly divergent class lines of the 1980s. In Macdonald's phrase, the idea that some people are "nice" and others are "common" has "in real life given rise to more drama than all the gangsters in Chicago."[19] Henry King's Stella Dallas was perhaps the first film to deal with this reality, a reality as divergent as Stella's cottage in Millhampton and Helen Morrison's villa in an Eastern suburb of Utopia.

NOTES

1. Oral History.

2. Radio listeners during the period 1937-53 will doubtless remember the familiar organ solo introducing the show: "How Can I Leave Thee?" Then followed the announcer: "... a continuation on the air of the true-to-life story of mother love and sacrifice, in which Stella Dallas saw her own beloved daughter Laurel marry into wealth and society, and, realizing the differences in their tastes and worlds, went out of Laurel's life...." John Dunning (Tune in Yesterday [Prentice-Hall: Englewood Cliffs, 1976], pp. 568-570) observed that she dropped g's, used "ain't" and double negatives, had little school learnin' but a good stock of common sense which failed to save her from appalling problems. Anne Elstner, who played Stella for the entire run, became "the most distinctive character on daytime radio."

3. Ronald Bowers, "Stella Dallas," Magill's Survey of Cinema, III, p. 1049.

4. Among the titles are Mother o' Mine, Mother's Boy, Mother's Cry, The Goose Woman, The Greater Claim, Greater than Love, The Greatest Love of All, Motherhood: Life's Greatest Miracle, Where's My Wandering Boy Tonight?, and Some Mother's Boy.

5. Dwight Macdonald, "Notes on Hollywood Directors (as of 1933)," On Movies (Prentice-Hall: Englewood Cliffs, 1969), p. 87.

6. Ibid.

7. Frances Marion, Off with Their Heads (Macmillan: New York, 1972), p. 122.

8. Oral History.

9. Lois Moran. Interview with the author, December 8, 1983.

10. Oral History.

11. Oral History.

12. Moran interview, December 1983.

13. Oral History

14. Ibid.

15. Perry, p. 581.

16. Letter to Samuel Goldwyn, n.d., reprinted in the Invitation to the Premiere of Stella Dallas, November 16, 1925.

17. Jack Alicoate, Associate Editor, Film Daily. This telegram and the ones following are in the collection of Mrs. Henry King.

18. Oral History.

19. Macdonald, p. 88.

Framed by the window, Laurel (Lois Moran) and Richard Grosvenor (Douglas Fairbanks, Jr.) make their vows, oblivious of Laurel's mother outside.

The pastoral in America's heartland: Janet Gaynor performing bucolic chores in *State Fair* (1932).

Chapter 5
State Fair: American Archetypes

In 1932 the Fox Film Corporation was in serious financial straits. From a high of 80, Fox stock was to bottom out at 0.75. As if in response to the crisis, Winfield Sheehan, its capable production executive, was vacationing in Europe. As the Depression worsened, frantic executives rushed Will Rogers, Fox's most magnetic male star, into three consistently disappointing pictures; speculation surfaced that the studio had killed Rogers.

King's career at Fox had begun auspiciously two years before, directing Will Rogers in Lightnin', a remake of a John Ford film: he had completed two other remakes in the interim--the greatly successful (and greatly sentimental) Merely Mary Ann (1931), an Israel Zangwill story starring Janet Gaynor; and a minor masterpiece, Over the Hill (1931), which combined an innovative approach to sound with John Seitz's chiaroscuro photography. Both films had been made 11 years earlier. Now King was assigned his fourth remake, The Woman in Room 13, an old stage play previously filmed in 1920. King's heart could not have been in the production, for Variety complained about the uninspired direction and found the story "a series of labored big acting scenes, desperately contrived, and they fool nobody."[1]

Fox's problems were compounded by the fact that in 1932, the magic was rapidly fading from the once immensely popular Janet Gaynor-Charles Farrell duo, and after seven films that team no longer insured the success of a picture. Everyone recognized that some changes were needed as falling figures at the box office sounded the alarm.

King was looking around for something worthy of his energies, a project he could believe in. Then in the spring of that year he read Phil Stong's delightful and moving little novel about an Iowa farm family who leave home to spend a week at the Iowa Fair. He loved the book, but the studio under the present confused regime was not particularly interested. The executives he had to deal with would not read it, and he was not eager to make a picture under their aegis anyway. He decided to telegraph an offer to purchase the book himself if the studio turned it down. Then King took a leave of absence for a few weeks.

He returned to the studio just at the time Sheehan was coming back from Europe. Sheehan was enthusiastic: "I have bought it. Dismiss whatever else you have on your mind and take on State Fair. What do you want?" King immediately suggested his favorite actor whose friendship he had so enjoyed in Lightnin': "I want Will Rogers." But Sheehan was adamant: "No. Absolutely not."[2]

King, however, had planted the seed. In consultation with Sol Wurtzel, Fox's production chief for programmers, Sheehan decided that the novel had the makings of a major hit. Sheehan called King one Sunday morning and asked him to come out to the studio. "We have a suggestion," Sheehan told him. "If you take Rogers, we want you to take Janet Gaynor, Spencer Tracy, and Sally Eilers--everyone we have in the studio."

"I'd be silly not to accept it," King replied.[3]

"Everyone in the studio" meant the brightest lights in the Fox firmament. Gaynor was badly in need of a new partner; Rogers would find his career revived with a solid role in a good story. Janet Gaynor in 1932 had won much the same kind of following that had established Mary Pickford as "America's Sweetheart." Her star was born in 1927 when Fox teamed her with Farrell in Borzage's Seventh Heaven; she again shone luminously in Murnau's Sunrise (1927), a film which has been called a perfect picture, and the last effloresence of the silents. The first actress to receive an Oscar, Gaynor had reigned at the box office longer than any other current feminine star except Garbo and Pickford (who failed to make a successful transition to sound). As a contract player (she was Sheehan's personal protegée), she said that she never worried about how her films were doing, whether she was more successful in the South than in the North (as has been averred), or whether she was being overexposed by Fox.[4] Sheehan personally chose the role of Margy for her and asked King to take it to her as "a little present." Over the weekend, she read it and called back to say she was delighted with the part.

If an average American were asked in 1932 to name a national hero, Will Rogers' name would surely have ranked among the most mentioned. More than an entertainer, Rogers was homo americanus, one-quarter Indian, and a living example of the democratic experience, perhaps the most popular American sage since Benjamin Franklin. His views were widely listened to, and his voice was thought to be significant in the election of Roosevelt that year. Everyone over 60 has a vivid recollection of Rogers; but today he is only a name except to those who know the culture of the 1920s and 30s. In State Fair he was to reveal the folksy reality of a next-door neighbor or a favorite uncle.

Spencer Tracy, then under contract with Fox, was to be cast as the crooked concession operator, but before he could be engaged, another project prevented his taking the assignment and the part went to Victor Jory, now playing in his second film. For Pat Gilbert, the newspaper reporter, Sheehan and King decided to cast a a young actor who two years before in Lewis Milestone's All Quiet on the Western Front had moved audiences thoughout the world with his sensitive performance as the German soldier who dies reaching for a butterfly. At 24 Lew Ayers also projected with that sensitivity a certain melancholy: he would be perfect as the newspaperman with a touch of wistful experience of women and the world.[5]

Sally Eilers, rising rapidly after her discovery at Hollywood's Fairfax High in 1928 (where she was a friend and classmate of Carole Lombard's), had appeared for King opposite James Dunn in Over the Hill, and most recently in one of the top pictures of 1931, Frank Borzage's Bad Girl, in which she had been a sensation. Flo Ziegfeld was reputed to have called her "the most beautiful girl I've ever seen," and Chaplin thought she would make him a marvelous leading lady. Her bright good looks, which were more sophisticated than ingenuous, were just right for Emily, the aerial artiste who knows the ropes as well as the high wires.

Teaming with Rogers was his popular co-star, the warmly maternal Louise Dresser, an Edwardian beauty who had starred in roof garden musicals produced by Dillingham, Frohman, and Lew Fields. She had played opposite Valentino in The Eagle (1925) and had received spectacular notices for her role in The Goose Woman that same year. After that performance, maternal roles became her forte, and she had the title role opposite Jolson in Mammy (1930). In 1930 she had teamed with Rogers in Lightnin',--the first of seven pictures she was to make with the great Fox star. She was now 49; Picture Play Magazine, unaccountably overlooking MGM's Marie Dressler, called her "the only feminine star of the sunset years."

For the role of Wayne, the teenage son who has spent the winter throwing his mother's embroidery hoops in the tool shed to perfect his skills so that he can win prizes at the Fair next summer, the assignment went to Norman Foster who seemed at 32 a little old for a fresh-faced farm youth; but his performance was thoroughly credible, and creditable enough to ensure him prominent roles for a few years (notably in John Ford's Pilgrimage that same year). Foster later went on to become a "B" film director specializing in Mr. Moto and Charlie Chan pictures.

King started immediately into script preparation. Paul Green, the young North Carolina playwright whose House of Connolly was a Broadway success (and which King would film as Carolina in 1934), agreed to write the opening--all he had time for, as he had to leave for the East within the fortnight. Sonya Levien, the capable young scenarist who had given Rogers two of his best films, They Had to See Paris and So This Is London, and who had delivered other hits to Fox in 1931-32, collaborated with King in fashioning the balance of the script.[6] She was later to team with King to bring in two box-office winners in The Country Doctor (1936) and In Old Chicago (1938). The novel laid itself out beautifully for treatment, as King's notes and marginalia indicate. King rearranged dialogue, making such notes to himself as "Here

Pat and Margy must get something in common" and eliminated Wayne's episodes with Emily at the race track and at dinner to substitute the dialogue in the hotel room: "Start last eveng. Scene here." For the chapter on Farmer Frake's prize-winning boar, Blue Boy, King noted "Excellent Sequence."

Every best seller pre-sells to some extent a motion picture in that it creates an audience. State Fair was a best seller in this country and was syndicated in papers with such diverse markets as San Francisco, Sacramento, Philadelphia, Pittsburgh, Minneapolis, Kansas City and Cleveland. It reached across to old and young, to rural and metropolitan audiences. King, having been raised on a farm, instinctively knew how to retain the freshness of the novel and the broad appeal in translating the property to the screen.

To begin with, the presentation of the credits promises something original and fresh. To the swelling strains of the film's delightful theme song, "Romantic," a book opens to announce the cast of characters (only eight); a page turns next to the title "Henry King's production of"; the page turns again to a large billboard which passersby have stopped to look at, bearing in bold face clarendon the words STATE FAIR. Sweepers wash the board with their brushes to reveal the screenplay by Sonya Levien and Paul Green, the novel by Phil Stong; and so on.

The opening scene bears the signature of a Henry King film. On Abel Frake's farm it is late afternoon. Across the pleasant landscape, the camera pans to reveal a meadow, a stream, a large and comfortable frame house with a vine-covered porch and a white picket fence, and--after these promising poetic touches--a hog pen where the snuffling grunts of a dozen animals overcome the opening music. Abel Frake (Will Rogers) is worried; he tastes the feed reserved for Blue Boy. It won't do, it's too musty. Where is that Storekeeper who's making a special trip to bring Blue Boy fresh chow? Frake anxiously waits, like a father expecting a doctor for an ailing child. In the large kitchen, Melissa Frake (Louise Dresser), stopping doubtfully every now and then to sample her concoction, is busy stirring mincement in a large stoneware bowl. Margy (Janet Gaynor) is seated at a kitchen table printing labels for Melissa's pickles, for the pickles and the mincement and Blue Boy will all be entered in the appropriate categories tomorrow at the Fair. By the tractor in the barn Wayne is practicing to be a winner in the ring-toss game that bilked him of several dollars at last year's Fair.

These are the opening shots which offer another version of the pastoral in Henry King's America. Although in 1932 he probably would not then have employed the word, he recognized years later the interest of the film as "real Americana."[7] The country, King was to reflect, is just as important as the character,[8] and despite the fact that the film was shot on the Fox back

The Frake family taking their ease on a summer afternoon: Melissa (Louise Dresser) with her sewing, Able (Will Rogers, Sr.) reading his paper. Margy (Janet Gaynor) and Wayne (Norman Foster) are receiving some parental words of wisdom.

lot, there is an authentic Midwestern feeling about the picture. King made a special trip to Des Moines in the summer of 1932 to obtain extensive process plates to be integrated with the studio sequences.[9] The sense of a particular time and place inheres in such details as visiting on a front porch, iced tea, Margy's cooling herself with a palmetto fan in the kitchen, the oil cloth on the table, the pie safe, and the polished woodstove. Outside we hear the arrival of the Storekeeper who always keeps chains on his tires in case there's mud on the roadways.

"Poetic" is probably not a word King would have used about his own work; but it is a fitting adjective to describe the mood of the family on the summer evening of their journey to the Fairgrounds 125 miles away. In order to escape the heat of the day, they are travelling at nightfall, driving through tall rows of corn flanking the road on either side. King starred a sentence in Stong's novel: "The moon, last light of humanity, was sinking in the east."[10] In the film, Margy's face is silhouetted against the moon which hangs low in the cornfields. Melissa muses, "Everything is so quiet. Seems like we are the last people in the world." The parents are in the front; the children sit with their backs to the cab; Blue Boy sleeps in his crate at the tailgate.

King was indebted to Stong for help with dialogue and visualization of the setting in a passage of the novel he marked "Ride to the Fair--Washed but not Curried." It goes like this...

> Driving alone in times as their forefathers had driven in the space of the Iowa prairies, they felt a sense of adventure and the large <u>Sehnsucht</u> of a starry, slightly humid Iowa night.
>
> "What are you thinking about, Margy?"
>
> "I'm not thinking about anything. I wish we were there. I wish it was morning."

Melissa suggests that Margy lie down...

> "There's plenty of room on top of that crate and [Blue Boy's] got some kind of a bed fixed up there."
>
> "And sleep over that hog? No, thank you."
>
> Abel laughed. "That's a special hog. It isn't everybody that gets a chance to sleep on the crate of a hog like that. Besides, he's been washed and curried till he's probably cleaner than any of us. We've been washed, but we haven't been curried."
>
> "I don't like hogs," said Margy decisively.
>
> "Well," said her father, "maybe hogs don't like you, either, but you don't hear Blue Boy making a big fuss because you're riding in his car." [So clearly are

> these the accents of Will Rogers that it is difficult to imagine another actor playing the part.][11]

Abel turns the radio on for some gentle night music, 1930s style. Abel helps Melissa cover herself with a shawl. Melissa smiles. Wayne is asleep. Margy stares pensively into the moon-dappled shadows. Abel surveys his family and contentedly reflects, "Blue Boy likes it."

This journey is no ordinary trip. It is an archetype of the journey. Each member, Abel and Melissa, Wayne and Margy, is now ready to set out upon a personal quest. Abel Frake is out to prove that he can raise the best and the largest Hampshire boar in the state of Iowa, thus evidencing his worth and prowess as a farmer. As his name indicates, he relates to an agrarian vocation. Melissa comes of pioneer stock, among whom is her great-grandmother who defended herself from Indians; she feels a keen connection to the past which she keeps alive in twice-told tales to the family. Melissa's goal is to demonstrate the quality of that heritage in her version of the family recipes for mincemeat and pickles.

For the younger generation, the Fair represents Experience in the Blakean sense. Ever since Christian, in Bunyan's Pilgrim's Progress, encountered the attractions of this world in his sojourn at Vanity Fair, the Fair in the cultural tradition of the West has represented a necessary stage of the questing spirit on its journey. For Blake, every human being must at some point in his or her psychic evolution leave the realm of Innocence, in which the soul is comfortably protected and knows not of evil, to gain knowledge by exploring the realm of Experience. In Experience, one must encounter evil as well as perils and temptations. The reward of Experience is knowledge vital to the psychic growth of the individual. To put it in a more mythic way, Experience is the tree of knowledge of good and evil, of which all mankind are destined to partake if a human being is to be autonomous rather than an automaton. So the journey for Margy and Wayne promises both risks and rewards, dangers no less than the dazzling excitements of novelty and the metropolis. This commentary is clearly in accord with the spirit of the picture as is evident from the opening sequence after the credits. The two figures of the Journey and the Fair converge in the epigraph, just before the story begins:

> A State Fair is like Life--begins lustily--offers everything--whether you go for sheep and blue ribbons--or shape and blue eyes. And too soon, it's all over!

More accurately, life is like a State Fair. One sets out to seek achievement and recognition and/or the adventure of love.

Metaphor gives meaning to life; and one tends to view life, however unconsciously, in terms of metaphor: of life as dream (Midsummer Night's Dream), as play (The Tempest), as game (Magister Ludi), as battle (The Bhagavad-Gita). In this book and film, the Fair offers the sojourn of Experience and a temporary destination in the journey of the questing spirit.

The structure of the journey is as old as mythology, and storytellers, whatever the form of the tale, necessarily draw upon the device. Sunrise, It Happened One Night, Stagecoach, The Grapes of Wrath, The Treasure of Sierra Madre, Night of the Hunter, Midnight Cowboy, and Apocalypse Now come immediately to mind, all pictures with identifiable literary antecedents. (Sullivan's Travels, La Strada, and 2001: A Space Odyssey on the other hand have no literary prototypes.) The structure requires that some kind of change take place in the psyche of the characters who undergo the journey, so that by the end they are not the same people they were in the beginning.

Every journey, therefore, is crossed with hazards and temptations. Odysseus and Aeneas must wander for years beset by perils and obstacles, and Dante's Pilgrim is warned that all who would visit the infernal depths should abandon hope. So Stong fashions a kind of Carlylean Nay-Sayer who will warn Abel at he beginning of his trip of the perils along the way. In Stong's words the Storekeeper believes "that Heaven ordains all things for the worst."[12] This role of genial pessimism was assigned to Frank Craven, a Broadway actor then making his second film; he would be remembered best for the role he began originally in the theatre in 1938--the stage manager in Sam Wood's version of Wilder's Our Town (1940). In a memo to King (October 26, 1932), Sheehan pointed out that the Storekeeper "should build up with a little comedy the risk, dangers, and perils of a trip to the State Fair which would reflect that Margy, Wayne, and Melissa were in danger."[13]

Thus the Storekeeper in serious jest admonishes: "There's just one thing you want to watch out for, Abel.... Don't let your hog get too good." If he's the best hog, the Storekeeper explains, he'll never win. After he warns of the possibility of hog cholera and pneumonia, Abel reminds him that he left out cyclones and earthquakes. Abel, however, takes the bet. The bet is that Blue Boy will win the sweepstakes, that they will all have a good time, and that they will all be better off for the experience when the Fair is over. Thus the wager in the book, as in the film, provides a pivotal point for the narrative and sets up a series of unifying expectations. Will Blue Boy win? Will they all have a good time? Will they truly be better off for the experience?

Margy is not certain what she wants, except she needs to learn about life; she seeks a knowledge larger than her protected girlhood on an Iowa farm has allowed. In a candid moment with her brother on the afternoon of their departure, Margy asks "Don't you ever want to go away somewhere and just raise hell?"[14] Although Harry Ware (Frank Melton) has been a friend since childhood, she finds his devotion to his dairy herd boring. She won't answer the phone for fear that she must talk to Harry. Harry comes anyway to impose his plans on their future. What if she doesn't marry him? she asks. It's the man who has to decide things, he tells her, but Margy can decide where their home is to be built. Her interest in him is obviously diminishing until the point where Harry begins to plan their honeymoon: Niagara Falls and Washington in cherry blossom time. "I'd almost marry you to make the trip" (a line sharpened by Sheehan from Stong's "I'd almost marry you to go along"). Margy, then, needs adventure and escape from familiar confinements: in a word, Experience.

Wayne is also ready for his rites of passage. On his last visit to the Fair, he suffered stinging humiliation when he squandered his savings in an attempt to win prizes in a ring-tossing concession. His one prize was a pearl-handled revolver of worthless pot metal. Wayne had shown the first attribute of Innocence in his inability to distinguish appearance and reality. Now he wants to show that he can make his way in a world of deception and traps by demonstrating the wits and skills necessary to triumph over the barker's worldly cunning.

There are dangers for Abel and Melissa too. Margy, observing her father's devotion to Blue Boy, wonders that he seems to think more of the boar than of his own children: "What if Blue Boy doesn't win, Mother?" she asks. Melissa, half-shaking her head, replies, "They'll have to shoot him!" As for Melissa, she stoutly refuses to put the brandy in the mincemeat until Abel points out, "If you're going to leave out something, and you're going to win a prize, you'd better leave out the mincemeat." When she leaves the kitchen, Abel pours a couple of cups of brandy into her recipe. When he's out of the room, Melissa changes her mind and pours in the rest of the bottle. Has the mincemeat now been ruined as a result of this double dose? Melissa, moreover, must face at the Fair her supremely confident antagonist Mrs. Metcalfe, who has established her reputation formidably as the favored entrant in the pickles and mincemeat division. Melissa fears that Mrs. Metcalf has entered the mincemeat competition to spite her.

In the motel-less world of 1932, King shows us in a grove near the Fairgrounds a tent city, a cheerful community of visitors who exchange news about family events and swap observations on past prizes and forthcoming entries. In the daytime there is *al fresco* dining and washing in an area lined with tables and shelves stacked with jars and dishes. At night the Frakes' tent is illuminated by a kerosene lamp which casts animated silhouettes as seen from outside. On the morning of the first day Abel is worried because Blue Boy won't eat; and if Blue Boy won't eat, Abel can't eat.

As Wayne wanders through the Fairgrounds, he hears hammers assembling concessions, and black workmen singing some work chanty. Bright canvasses announce a fat lady, a spider woman, tattooed ladies, a ventriloquist, a mind reader. A band marches across; a calliope plays; a snatch of jazz follows; blonde dancing girls kick up their heels. In rapid cuts appear the hardened faces of barkers whose raucous cries invite the crowd.

The stage is now set for Wayne's encounter with his nemesis from last year, the barker. Inspired casting assigned this role to Victor Jory.[15] The barker recognizes Wayne's skill with a smile of contempt. Would-he-step-right-up? Wayne flawlessly rings each prize he tries for, and the alarmed barker threatens to summon the police. At this point a woman steps forward to claim that her father is the inspector of police, a remark sufficiently intimidating to enable Wayne to collect his prizes and his money. Wayne is happy and satisfied; having bested the barker he offers to buy the helpful young woman dinner. She sizes up the young man with dewy-eyed interest: "I am not a wild woman or a tame one, but my tendencies are good," she lets him know. She can't join him now, but she can meet him that night at eight.

That night Wayne comes to the meeting place where a trapeze artist is to perform. He looks about him before realizing that the woman he is looking for is now standing above him. She steps forward and extends her arms, opening her cape like a pair of wings. She is the Queen of the Air as she ascends high above and steps into an illuminated swing. In Stong's novel, Emily is only the daughter of the owner of the travelling show. By making her an aerialist, the scenarists have associated Emily with a spiritual element. Emily is to be Wayne's teacher--in fact the barker presenting her tells the crowd that they bring her "for your amusement and education." Emily will initiate Wayne into the ways of the world when she offers him his first cocktail in Emily's rooms; but more significantly Emily is the older woman who will initiate him into love. That this initiation also has its spiritual aspects is evident when Emily declares that she will slip into something more comfortable. She emerges from her bedroom a moment later loosely clad in a satin kimono, apparently beltless and buttonless. As she turns to Wayne, her back moves to the camera. Adorning the kimono is an image universally associated with the transcendent: a gorgeous sequined butterfly fills the frame. Wayne's voice is heard: "I didn't suppose anyone could be so lovely." Fadeout.

Less obviously associated with the transcendent is Pat Gilbert, the young journalist tinged with a slight cynicism. For Margy he represents the unknown world. Has she not read his report of the last Geneva Peace Conference that almost started a war? Or his stories on the Bolshevik farmers of the Midwest? Or his interview with Mussolini? She doesn't pick up the irony of his questions, but they find a common topic to bring them together, the Storekeeper who was the subject of an interview. Pat is also her teacher, for Margy is not in her element when she stands up in fright on the roller-coaster; he saves her life, and he helps her overcome her fear. "Come on, stranger," he teases, "you can believe everything I tell you--everything." When Margy admits to never having been up in "an aeroplane swing," Pat tells her "I'll take you right up in the clouds."

Moonlight and clouds whirl by Margy and Pat while in the background a male quartet of quavering countertenors sings in close harmony the charming theme song, "Romantic." The whole scene barely lasts 40 seconds, but its lyrical quality is so joyous that one hardly realizes its brevity. When Margy the next morning tells Wayne of the roller-coaster ride, she exclaims, "You feel as if you're going right up to Heaven."

The testing of Melissa's pickles and mincement will be in a sense the testing of Melissa's skills as an Iowa homemaker after months of preparation and years of coming to the Fair. In the pavilion where hundreds of women are assembled, the camera pans to reveal shelf after shelf stacked with Mason jars of jams, preserves, and condiments. An irate lady complains bitterly, "No! No! No! My crabapple under my raspberry!" Melissa overhears a neighbor tell the redoubtable Mrs. Metcalfe that there's hardly any reason for the rest of them to enter, "since you're always sure to win."

Sheehan was responsible for a delightful embellishment to this scene. In his memo to King of October 25th, he wished to elevate the taste-test to a ceremony with elaborate ritual, thereby pointing up a contrast between the solemnity of the judges and the relatively commonplace act of tasting. To this end he suggested that the clerk with the ledger should look like a divinity student with gold spectacles; and the ritual of spraying the throat with the atomizer should be conducted "with the pomp, dignity, and importance of a college professor handing out diplomas." He also thought that the testing of the mincement should resemble a French wine-testing which had come across as very funny in a recent news reel: "This subject got its great comedy reaction from the smacking of the lips." The audience heard the smacking and watched the judges attempting to extract lingering flavors and then rolling their tongues about their lips. They also "rolled their eyes around when they tested the wine... like a jury reaching a great verdict when a man's life is at stake."

Dressed in wing collars, the three judges and the young clerk are impressively dignified. The young clerk with a towel over his arm carries an atomizer like a censer, and also opens his mouth when he sprays the judges' mouths. But the judges hardly taste Melissa's sweet pickles, her best entry she thinks. Mrs. Metcalf preens herself in anticipation. When the judges announce the winners in the three categories of Sour, Sweet, and Mixed, Melissa makes a clean sweep, and Mrs. Metcalf of Pittsville for her hubris gets Second Place. In the Mincemeat Division, the judges are led to Melissa Frake's entry by the aroma emitted from the stoneware crock. Having won the Grand Plaque for Exceptional Mincemeat, she tells Margy, "I've got the most that any woman can get in life."

Although King was delighted with Stong's handling of the Hampshire Boar Competition, he and Levien improved upon the episode significantly. By this point Abel's psychic investment in Blue Boy's winning has been well established, as well as the sympathetic relationship of Abel to the Boar's health and disposition. Abel tells Melissa that he knows why she wants Blue Boy to win--"then I'll be fit to live with for another year."

When the great day arrives, Abel is tending the ailing boar in his pen; he tells Blue Boy he knows he's not sick, just pretending. Over the loudspeaker he hears the announcement that the Grand Championship for Hamphire Boars will be held in Pavillion Number One. Blue Boy lies down with a snort. A band enters,[16] followed by three judges, the chief of whom almost equals Blue Boy in porcine girth. Back in the grandstands, the Frake family fretfully wait while the judges solemnly enter. In dramatic close-up, Congressman Goodheart intones in the orotund accents of old-fashioned oratory: "During this great day of Boar judging, you have seen hundreds of seemingly perfect boars eliminated...." The first boar, Whirlwind, enters to applause; but where's the other contestant? And, Melissa anxiously asks, "Where's Pa?" Then the announcer introduces Blue Boy, but the Frakes stop applauding when they notice Blue Boy looking down--"depressed about something." Blue Boy shuffles off to a corner, and the judges make only a brief inspection. As the judges leave to examine the other entry, Abel's face falls. But through the fence in his corner Blue Boy espies the red-haired Esmeralda.[17] The presence of Esmeralda infuses sudden vitality into the downcast boar, an energetic charge wittily conveyed in a series of rapidly accelerating crosscuts between the two. As his snout lifts and his spirits rise, the judges return to examine Blue Boy. "I never saw such poise!" "What a stance!" One judge (Hobart Cavanaugh, an oft-used player in King pictures) executes a dance-like series of movements as he moves up and down and around the boar.[18] Blue Boy wins, and Abel is happily accepting congratulations when a fight breaks out between the First and Second Place winners.[19]

It is the last night of the Fair. Wayne and Emily enter Emily's darkened room, their figures silhouetted against the window. As he embraces her, he murmurs, "I can't believe anything so wonderful could happen to me." Emily reminds him that this is their last evening. "Don't you believe it," he protests. "Don't think I'm going to let you slip away from me now." Emily breaks away; as if to dispel the enchantment, she switches the lights on.

"You mean you don't love me?" he asks.

"If I loved you when I first saw you as I do now, if I had known how true you are, I'd never have brought us--you and me--together. I do love you, Wayne, but I wouldn't marry you for anything in the world." Stong ends the scene with commentary King could not show: "He stepped across the thin, infinite border between boyhood and manhood...."

Cut sharply to Pat and Margy. Pat, having confessed to a womanizing past, nevertheless asks Margy to marry him. Margy reminds him that he would tie himself down, and there would be no more adventures for him. As for herself, there is someone at home; as a farm wife she would know how to be useful. In the following scene they walk slowly back to the campsite through the glen where they first declared their love. In the distance are heard the confused noises of music and barkers reminding the crowds that it is the last night. The strains of "Auld Lang Syne" sound from the Fairgrounds. "I love you, Pat," Margy says, "but sometimes you seem like something I'll wake up from." "Well," he replies, "I guess there's nothing more to say unless you say it." She looks at him as if about to say something, then breaks away in tears, turning back once more at the campground to look at him.

The scene opens the next morning with a tent collapsing to reveal Wayne standing dejectedly as the truck is readied for departure. Margy sits quietly in the back. They pass through the Fairgrounds, past workers hauling down equipment and the loaded carnival trailers standing about. "For goodness' sake," exclaims Melissa, "you don't seem like the same youngsters that came to the Fair with us."

The novel ends with the parents happily returning to Brunswick, for Abel wins his bet, and the children not so happy but somehow the richer for having tasted the strange bittersweet fruit of experience.

King shows us Margy looking morosely from her bedroom window, indifferently agreeing to her mother's summons that she come out on the porch for some iced tea. Wayne guesses that he'll drop by to see his girl Eleanor and stay for supper. The Storekeeper has arrived. How was the Fair? "Swell," answers Wayne as he leaves the house. "All had a good time," Abel tells him. In the background is heard the ominous and repeated sound of thunder. But the Storekeeper, who sees Margy standing withdrawn and alone, wonders, "Maybe something happened that we don't know about? Did _you_ have a good time, Margy?" Before she can answer, the phone rings. Cross cut to Margy in front of an old wall telephone: "I do, Pat! You are? Yes, Yes, Yes." She rushes onto the porch where the Storekeeper asks her again if she had a good time. "The best! The happiest of my life!" The rain begins to fall hard and Margy runs out into the downpour, across the yard, into the highway, stopping before a billboard announcing the State Fair. A car pulls up and Pat gets out to take Margy, her hair streaming in the rain, into his arms. Behind them the falling rain peels the bright advertisements of racing horses and beautiful ladies to reveal two words never more engagingly disclosed--The End.

Sheehan had wisely enjoined in his memorandum: "At the finish you have to show the girl with Ayres. I want to see them in each other's arms at the end--big clinch." It was just the right ending: it was credible, but even more important it was the classically comic finale that celebrates love whose purpose is to make life go on.

State Fair was a test for more than the four characters; it was a test of Fox's survival. In the midst of production Sheehan came out to the set one day and called Rogers and Gaynor and King together--Fox's two top stars and a principal director who was at that time earning $4,000 per week. Their combined salaries were a sizeable chunk of the studio's payroll. Sheehan said soberly, "We're at a point where we can't meet the payroll, and we want to know what you'll do to help." The three immediately volunteered to defer their salaries; after all, the depth of the Depression was a time when teachers and government workers were being paid in scrip. King remembered Rogers telling Sheehan, "I'm perfectly willing to put aside my salary if it will keep you from firing a lot of gatemen, policemen and secretaries. I can do without the money a lot better than they can." It was an entirely characteristic remark.

Fox survived that terrible year because of State Fair and Cavalcade, both Box Office Champions for 1933.[20] By 1934-35, the Motion Picture Almanac reported State Fair as 29th among All-Time Box Office successes. In the trade press, Film Daily correctly predicted (January 27, 1933) that the film would appeal where ever it is shown, big cities or small towns. It was "genuine entertainment" in which Rogers was "superb" and King's direction "outstanding." "Janet Gaynor was never seen to better advantage." Variety (January 31, 1933) praised the production for "the charm of naturalness and the virtue of sincerity" in this "straightforward story of a rural family that find their great moments at the State Fair." The picture would give Gaynor a fresh hold on her fans and would certainly not hurt Ayres whose flippant style was "a needed tang" for Gaynor's too sweet romantic interests of the past. The New York Times (January 30, 1933) considered that "watching this film is almost as interesting as going to a state fair, for nothing seems to be neglected during the week in which it is supposed to take place... a homey tale."

It was the last picture King was to direct for Rogers. He was a joy to work with, King remembered, for he never had to act: he was the part he played. Even Miss Gaynor, a big star in her own right, was "completely awed" by her association with him. Rogers would amuse the entire cast and crew between scenes by reading them his daily column as it came out of the typewriter.[21]

King and Rogers enjoyed a mutual respect and a strong friendship until the very end, when King visited Rogers on the eve of his fatal flight to Alaska with Wiley Post in 1934. For King, Rogers turned in a performance never exceeded in his other works, although perhaps equalled in James Cruze's David Harum (1934); his role in State Fair certainly surpassed his last work in John Ford's Steamboat 'Round the Bend (released posthumously, 1935). Rogers, who was greatly affected by the death of Marie Dressler in 1934, once told David Butler that "there is a permanent record of her on these talking pictures, and she'll always be with us. Don't worry, Old Will himself will always be there, unless they get tired of me."[22]

State Fair will also be there, for it is a permanent record of a time in rural America affectionately observed and delightfully realized. King and Levien's script provided the basis for two remakes in 1945 and 1962. But charming as is Walter Lang's 1945 version with an extensive musical score by Rodgers and Hammerstein, his picture lacks the simplicity and immediacy of the first; and the second remake (under José Ferrer) was a bad mistake. King's State Fair remains as American as the Fourth of July, yet now sadly forgotten and unjustly eclipsed by its musical successors.

King had turned in for Fox two all-time-grossers in State Fair and Merely Mary Ann, a film which by 1934-35 would number 54th in terms of box-office receipts since tabulation began. He now turned his attention to I Loved You Wednesday (1933), an interesting failure if for no other reason than that he forgot his own dictum about telling a story clearly. There followed Carolina (1934), a lost picture which was financially successful; and Marie Galante (1934), a film which might well have succeeded critically and financially if studio heads had not insisted on a happy ending. One More Spring (1935) is a Depression picture, but unlike La Cava's My Man Godfrey and Borzage's A Man's Castle with which it is often compared, its tender moments against the coldness of the time were not warm or frequent enough to ensure success with the public. His last film for the old Fox studio was a beautiful and heartfelt version of Way Down East (1935), a film which is emphatically not imitative of Griffith, the ice floe sequence excepted.

When Darryl F. Zanuck obtained control of the studio and merged Twentieth-Century Pictures with the Fox Film Corporation, King found a talented and exciting producer who infused him with a new energy. By the end of the decade this fruitful collaboration produced Twentieth-Century Fox's biggest moneymakers. Twentieth-Century Fox's golden years were ahead, and King, more than any other director, helped to make them.

NOTES

1. Oral History. King once called The Woman in Room 13 "the worst picture I ever made," but The Seventh Day (1922) and This Earth is Mine (1959) are surely better candidates for this distinction. The Woman in Room 13 at least moves, and there is a promising election sequence and montage at the opening. Moreover, both Ralph Bellamy and Elissa Landi give lively performances in this melodrama of blackmail, suicide, and sacrifice. As a professional, King thought it his duty to do his best with each assignment given to him.

2. Oral History.

3. Ibid.

4. Janet Gaynor. Interview with the author, November 25, 1983. She thought Farrell did not make the transition to sound so easily: her pictures without him were successful; his without her were not.

5. According to King's recollections in the Oral History project, and from the evidence of a scrap of paper on which he jotted down the names of actors for the cast, Robert Montgomery of MGM was originally under consideration for the Pat Gilbert role.

6. Phil Stong wrote in letter to King (dated November 2, 1932) that "the work on the script has made my writing clearer and more objective--I think that ten or twelve weeks of moving pictures are probably an excellent thing for a writer." But Stong's studio work is not credited in the film (possibly because, as King Vidor maintained, Stong's wife was the talent and basically the writer of the family). King, known for his magnanimity and modesty, was never one to withhold recognition.

7. Letter to Stella Hartwig Pence (August 4, 1975).

8. Henry King at Claremont, videotape, 1977.

9. This footage taken at the Iowa State Fair held in Des Moines (where King also arranged for the purchase of the Duke of Rosedale, that year's prize-winning boar) was then projected through a screen behind the actors--thus Wayne in the studio appeared to be walking down the Midway. At least one location sequence--the tent city--was filmed in Sacramento at the California State Fair.

10. Phil Stong, State Fair (The Century Co.: Philadelphia, 1932), p. 60.

11. Ibid.

12. Stong, November 1932 letter.

13. This memorandum and the subsequent ones cited were found folded in King's own marked copy of Stong's novel.

14. In a letter (November 1, 1932) written by James Wingate, representing the Association of Motion Picture Producers, the movie industry's self-regulating censorship organization

headed by Will Hays, it was pointed out to Sheehan that AMPP had a number of problems with the script. These included two "damns," a "Lord," and a "Hell." Sheehan on November 3 asked King to comply with the code. Although two "profane" citations were excised, King evidently stood firm on two uses, including Abel's exclamation over Blue Boy: "Lord have mercy!"

15. Jory played the lead in King's unsuccessful I Loved You Wednesday (1935), but his best-known part was that of the would-be rapist on the staircase in Gone With the Wind.

16. Originally the band was to have played "Land of Hope and Glory," which King had actually heard at the Iowa State Fair. In a memo to King dated October 28, 1932, Julian Johnson, story editor for Fox, objected to this choice in view of Fox's forthcoming major release of Cavalcade, Noel Coward's play about three generations of an upper-class English family.

17. At one time in the script the sow was called Clara, but after Julian Johnson's objection that it looked like a bad crack at Clara Bow, the name Esmeralda was retained from the novel.

18. Doubtless King picked up a point from Sheehan's memo in which he pointed out that "great comedy... can be obtained out of the solemnity, study, and angle at which the judges stand and the poses they assume when they are judging the pigs."

19. King arranged to buy the three champion hogs at the Iowa State Fair. He wanted an understudy in the event that one should be hurt in the fight. He also arranged for a Professor of Animal Husbandry from Iowa State to accompany the animals on their train ride across the country.

20. Warner Brothers pulled through the crisis with Gold Diggers of 1933 and 42nd Street; Paramount stayed afloat with She Done Him Wrong and I'm No Angel; RKO had the big picture of the year, King Kong, with Little Women in second place at that studio.

21. King's letter to Dale Hornung, Detroit, Michigan (January 30, 1973). Miss Gaynor, recollecting in the November 1983 interview, also remembers these readings. She was surprised to learn at the time of casting that she would receive top billing in the picture, such was her reverence for Rogers.

22. P. J. O'Brien, Will Rogers (John C. Winston Co.: Philadelphia, 1935), p. 84. Ironically, the film exists today only because Rogers kept a personal print from which in 1969 the Museum of Modern Art made a duplicate negative. The studio neglected to preserve the film, the original negative of which was destroyed by fire in 1933.

Abel Frank (Will Rogers) looks on as two judges (Hobart Cavanaugh is at the right) assess the merits of Blue Boy (the prize-winning Hampshire boar Duke of Rosedale).

"But, sirs, you can't do this!": The James Gang stage their first robbery aboard the St. Louis Midland Railway.

Chapter 6
Jesse James: A True Story

Nunnally Johnson first began working on Jesse James in 1936; but he had been thinking of the story ever since he had seen as a small boy in Georgia the Jewel Kelly Stock Company perform an old melodrama called The James Boys in Missouri. The scene which had indelibly imprinted itself on his mind is at the end: Jesse is taking down the sampler, Bob Ford is taking aim from behind, and small boys in the audience are screaming for him to "watch out for the dirty little coward." Although the play was ultimately forgotten, what is significant is that for the key scene in the script Johnson drew upon a theatrical source rather than history.[1]

There were a number of versions in the developing screenplay. Johnson and Curtis Kenyon, who had provided the story for Lloyds of London, came up with a new narrative with one notable strength: a character based on a newspaper editor, Major John Edwards of Sedalia, Missouri, whose partisan editorials helped shape James' image. After laying the script aside for a year, Johnson now collaborated with Gene Fowler, the well-known journalist of the 1930s and 40s, and with another Fox writer, Hal Long; this version cast the railroad as the chief antagonist and succeeded in making the outlaws sympathetic.

Fowler and Long used Zerelda (or Zee), Jesse's sweetheart, as a decoy to lure Jesse into town where she is imprisoned by the local town boss, Will Wallace. Jesse's men in this version are dressed as mourning women and in this disguise will spring her from jail. Zanuck found this complication unsatisfactory and suggested instead that Jesse should give himself up, at which point Jesse would discover that the railroad had framed him. The episode in which Frank James audaciously comes to rescue his brother was borrowed from a French thriller Johnson had seen on the New York stage in the 1920s; in that play, The Purple Mask, the hero insists that he will kidnap the prefect of police at midnight.[2] With this additional episode Johnson at last had a satisfactory script in the fourth revision.

As Nora Johnson reports, when her father Nunnally took the script to King, King's response was immediate--he wanted to do it.[3] It was not the first time Johnson and King had worked together, as Johnson had helped prepare the story and helped produce The Country Doctor (1936), a smash hit for the newly-formed Twentieth-Century Fox Film Corporation.[4] The two men shared a similar Southern heritage and knew what it was like to grow up in a small town. Johnson could trust King to treat his material with respect. (That was not an assumption he could make about John Ford whose treatment of Johnson's screenplay of Tobacco Road [1941], the blockbuster novel and play by Erskine Caldwell, would leave him appalled.[5])

Although King at this time was eager to do Jesse James, Zanuck was pushing King to make Stanley and Livingston. King voiced strong objection to the script as then written; and Zanuck, in King's words, "got mad as hell." But he gave into King, even though he didn't share King's conviction that Jesse James would make a big picture. Zanuck argued, "You want to do Jesse James? You do Jesse James. That's fine! You and Nunnally go ahead and do Jesse James! You've been doing these big pictures that are box-office attractions all over the world. Jesse James will be good in Tennessee, southern Illinois, and Arkansas and Missouri, a few places like that."[6] Overlooking Zanuck's grumpy reservations, King started preparing Jesse James, but then he laid the project aside for six months while he brought in Alexander's Ragtime Band. When that was completed, Zanuck was ready to give Jesse James priority.

King undertook preparation with his customary painstaking research. He flew to Missouri and located Frank James' son in Kearney. For several days they talked. They visited the house where Jesse had lived, and in the garden they sat under the tree which shaded Jesse's grave. All the information he thought relevant he passed on to Johnson who incorporated what he could use.[7]

King then took Johnson's completed script and flew to Florida where he rented a house on a beach, isolating himself from everyone except a cleaning man. His schedule was to get up every morning, run down to the beach, swim for a while, and then work until dinner. Without interruption he worked steadily for 10 days, so that he could plan every detail and visualize scenes and movements. He could thus save time to help develop performances and needful bits of business. King then flew to Bartlettsville, Oklahoma, where he met his trusted assistant director Robert Webb, and they took off in King's Waco cabin plane to scout locations. The actual settings in Kearney, where King had interviewed Robert James, and Liberty, where the James brothers had lived, were now so urbanized, so crossed with power lines and obstructed by billboards, that King knew the country would not be adaptable. They continued searching until a friend suggested they could find unspoiled locales in Pineville, Missouri.[8] They rented a car and toured the rustic byways of the Ozarks. In Pineville they found Mayor Drumm mowing the courthouse lawn.

At King's behest, the mayor assembled the city and civic leaders together for dinner at a limestone cave in the mountains. King acted as the host. King explained his purpose and some of the implications of making a major picture in Pineville. "Now understand," he said, "a man is not going to come in with a camera to take pictures. You're going to think Ringling Brothers, Barnum and Bailey Circus is coming when you see a whole trainload come in here from all over the country."[9] King promised he would give Pineville a definite date as soon as he had worked out a budget and obtained studio approval for the project. Many Pineville resident were skeptical and suspected city-slicker schemes; but the president of the Pineville Chamber of Commerce knew that King was in earnest and that it would be the biggest thing ever to hit Pineville.[10]

It now remained to secure location approval--not easily done because Zanuck had resisted locations ever since some director had taken a crew up to Oregon for snow scenes and then lost 10 days because of the snow. Zanuck had vowed, "I'll never let a company go on location again as long as I live! It'll all be made on the back lot."[11] But now Zanuck was on vacation in Europe, and William Goetz was acting studio head. When King took Goetz 16mm Kodachrome movies of such locales as a chink cabin, a pastureland with split rail fences, and the ante-bellum courthouse of rose-red brick, Goetz refused to interfere in any way and King's wishes were honored.[12] King then turned his pictures over to William Darling, the studio art director who had imparted such a fresh look to Way Down East and who had designed spectacular sets for In Old Chicago. Except for some indoor scenes and the climactic Northfield raid, all shooting was done on location. To the acutely discerning eye, Northfield bears some resemblance to the studio's familiar Western street in Movietone City; but the flight of the James brothers from Northfield is undertaken through Ozark country. The spectacular leap by the James brothers from the bluff into the lake, reputed to be the highest jump on horseback ever filmed, took place at the Lake of the Ozarks.[13]

The decision to shoot the picture on location was certainly aesthetically sound. The location infused the kind of authenticity simply not replicable elsewhere. In some cases extras were able to find clothes which had belonged to their grandparents.[14] King, whose films always show a loving care for period details in transportation, was able to find a Victorian locomotive and old passenger cars in a siding of the Dardanelle and Russellville Railroad in Arkansas.[15] He had the engine reconditioned in Meinhardt, Missouri, and the cars restored to a gleaming smartness. He supplemented local horse-drawn vehicles by ordering new surries and buggies from a coachmaker in Lawrenceville, Indiana.[16]

Despite these costly details, King made the claim (which seems somewhat unlikely) that Jesse James was able to bring in more money per dollar spent than any other film made up to that time. The film was budgeted for a whopping $1,165,242.72. Of this sum, $8,000 was to be paid to the James family (for story rights) to remove objections and satisfy their interests. Script development had cost $47,139.05. The allocation for cast salaries was budgeted at $128,079; but the largest single item was King's salary-- $75,000--while Nunnally Johnson as associate producer would receive $60,000.[17] Sets would come in at $53,700; wardrobe at $27,376; transportation at $4,874.75; and location costs at $70,421.18. A large item--$28,205--went for insurance; $53,700 for the transformation of Pineville into a nineteenth-century town; and $7,000 for the refurbishing and rental of the train and crew for the spectacular robbery. Although the film went slightly over budget by $26,509.73--an unusual phenomenon for a King picture--Zanuck could not have argued with the kind of block-buster success the picture created. For years after, however, Zanuck ribbed King about wanting to travel and see the world at studio expense.

Once Zanuck had made Jesse James a major production, there was no question that its star would be Tyrone Power. Only two years earlier he had been a mere $75 per week contract player, but he had had the resourcefulness to introduce himself to Henry King who had directed his father Tyrone Power, Sr., in Fury, a Richard Barthelmess vehicle of 1922. King was so impressed with the young man's bearing, assured manners, and striking good looks, that he was able to persuade Zanuck to let him test Power for the lead in the studio's prestige picture for 1936, Lloyds of London. When Zanuck agreed with King's estimate of the young actor's promise, Don Ameche (an earlier King discovery in Ramona) was removed and within months a new star shone over Hollywood.

Power handled a number of routine assignments as leading man blamelessly, and now as the protégé of both Zanuck and King, he was destined to star in Twentieth Century-Fox's big budget productions. In 1938 he was the leading man for two of King's sensationally successful pictures: In Old Chicago and Alexander's Ragtime Band. King developed a friendly regard for Power with whom he was to make 11 pictures. Jesse James was an excellent choice for the rising actor, enabling Power to show more than dazzling teeth and the long lashes which had made him a feminine heartthrob: he could ride, fight, smile and smoulder, as well as kiss Nancy Kelly in the somewhat passionless conventions of Hollywood osculation at that time. There was something of the bad boy in his role as Dion in In Old Chicago; in Jesse James this persona would be writ large.

The most problematic assignment was Frank James. Johnson had confessed to King the surprising information that he had written the role for himself. King thought that Johnson was joking, for a certain drollness about him was characteristic. Now at a conference one morning with King, Johnson, and the studio's casting head, Lou Shriber, Zanuck asked who was going to play

Frank James. Johnson, also an associate producer on the picture, and shortly to be the fourth highest-paid executive at the studio, began speaking and was naturally one to be listened to. He listed the characteristics of the part, and in King's recollection, "sort of inching himself up on the chair." King kept his silence and then broke in, "There's only one man in my mind who can really play Frank James." Everyone turned to him. Nunnally smiled and moved forward slightly and looked at King in great anticipation. Then King said, "Henry Fonda." Johnson's face fell.[18]

Zanuck became so angry that King half expected him to throw a book, for up to this point, Fonda's career at Twentieth-Century Fox had been uneven. He had begun promisingly enough in a film which the screenwriter Philip Dunne was to say was the typical Twentieth-Century Fox picture--The Farmer Takes a Wife (1935), essaying the same role which had brought him fame on Broadway. In King's beautiful remake of Way Down East (1935), Fonda's luminous sincerity shone so brightly that Rochelle Hudson's Anna Moore was, by contrast, dreadful, her characterization so inept that like Anna she would have sunk on the ice floe had not Fonda (as David Bartlett) picked her up as well as the picture. King blamed himself that Way Down East was not more convincing: there was a striking difference in Barthelmess's running up and down on cakes of ice in the Connecticut River and Fonda's jumping over cakes of paraffin on the back lot with the perspiration running down his face. Zanuck, however blamed Fonda and not the back lot, "This guy has no business playing that kind of part," Zanuck interjected. "I think he's a lousy actor. I wouldn't have him in anything. To me he just killed the picture." Zanuck seemed to be on the verge of saying, "Don't ever mention that guy's name to me again." Suddenly he relented. "Henry, I think you have something there. By golly, I never thought of that. See if Fonda is available."[19]

Zanuck could not have followed Fonda's career that closely, for he had done nothing to deserve such pejorative generalization. Certainly there were inconsequential roles in inconsequential pictures--a Lily Pons trifle, a Davis melodrama; but Fonda had appeared in two beautiful color films, Hathaway's The Trail of the Lonesome Pine (1936) and an English picture, Wings of the Morning (1937), and delivered fine performances in Lang's You Only Live Once (1937) and Wyler's Jezebel (1938).

Now it was Fonda's turn to decide. Meetings between him and Zanuck were short of being contemptuous. He also realized that Frank James was a secondary role. He trusted Henry Hathaway whom he turned to for advice. Hathaway told him to accept it, that Frank was a part of him.[20] It was. Fonda found that he could channel his talent into the character and forget about being a star. Despite, or perhaps because of, a newly acquired moustache and a skill at chewing tobacco, Fonda walked away with the picture. Years later, he recalled, he boarded a taxi in New York, and the driver called him Frank.[21] Nobody forgot Fonda's Frank James. King said that Fonda played the role as written. It established him at Fox, retaining him for four great roles in the next two years: Ford's Young Mr. Lincoln, Drums Along the Mohawk, The Grapes of Wrath, and of course, Lang's The Return of Frank James.[22] In 1940 he was borrowed by Paramount for Preston Sturges' delightful The Lady Eve.

King booked for his feminine lead a girl of 17 who had had long experience as a child actress on the stage and in film. Zerelda was Nancy Kelly's second recent film role, the first being the routine Submarine Patrol in which John Carradine had also been featured. With sculpted features and the cover-girl good looks which had made her a prominent model, she seemed destined for stardom, especially since King was to select her as leading lady in next year's prestigious Stanley and Livingston. Despite these auspicious starts, that stardom never materialized.

The rest of the cast was solid. The chiselled-featured Randolph Scott was cast as the other man in love with Zee; it was the usual reliable performance of Randolph Scott playing Randolph Scott, performances associated with quiet humor, deft timing, and gentlemanly strength. Henry Hull took the part of the irascible newspaper editor, Rufus Cobb; it was a long way from the intense title role of the 1935 horror film The Werewolf of London. For almost two years on Broadway, he had memorably developed Jeeter Lester in Caldwell's Tobacco Road. King had seen him on stage and told him that he wanted the same choleric intensity, "only more refined." His Rufus Cobb acts as comic relief and choric commentator.

The Jameses' antagonist is Donald Meek as Mr. McCoy, president of the St. Louis and Midland Railroad, whose vitriolic determination to destroy Jesse is unlike the obsequious timidity of his usual characterizations. Still to come next year would be his most famous role as a passenger in John Ford's Stagecoach. In McCoy's employment is Barshee, the ruthless heavy ably played by the stocky Brian Donlevy. Ahead of him would lie other Western roles in Union Pacific, Destry Rides Again, and the cruel sergeant in Beau Geste, all in the banner year of 1939. But it was John Carradine's unforgettably gaunt face, piercing blue eyes, and reverberating voice that made him forever memorable as "the dirty little coward who shot Mr. Howard," so that in a parade down Hollywood Boulevard not long after the film's release, he was hissed, booed and pelted and for years after inextricably associated with Bob Ford.

Rounding out the strong supporting cast were Jane Darwell, among the most sincere of King's long line of mothers; her warmth and integrity endeared her to audiences in mother roles. King had cast her as the pioneer woman who befriends the

Tyrone Power, Henry King, Nancy Kelly, and Henry Fonda enjoying a break in the filming of Jesse James (1939).

wandering Indian family in Ramona (1935); she was to win an Academy Award in 1940 as Ma Joad in Ford's The Grapes of Wrath. Slim Summerville was a familiar face, whom King had already used in The Country Doctor and whose gangling, hayseed manners had brought a special authenticity to Seth Holcomb in King's Way Down East. Summerville plays the apprehensive jailer who knows the James boys are "set in their ways." J. Edward Bromberg had made a reputation in New York's progressive Group Theatre and in Odets plays; he would be cast as the smilingly cheerful--and hence oddly sinister--operative George Remington.

For twentieth-century Americans, film images re-created the past so powerfully that they in effect become the past. Griffith, who was fully aware of the power of the image, went to painstaking detail to authenticate the look of interiors, so that for a generation of Americans to remember the Emancipation Proclamation was to recall Joseph Henaberry signing the document in the Oval Office; to think of the Battle of Petersburg was to remember Walthall's charging with the Confederate flag into the cannon; to think of the South's impoverishment was to remember Mae Marsh's "Southern ermine." To recall the historic moment when the coasts of the continent are linked by the golden spike in Utah was to remember DeMille's Union Pacific. In using these well-loved and familiar character players, King attached to the roles some of the actors' known personae (e.g., Scott, Meek, Darwell, Donlevy, Summerville, Carradine). The use of these actors, all of whom inherit a wealth of significant association from previous roles, extends the characters' legendary dimensions; they carry connotations well beyond the shaping function of any one movie or director, as John Ford surely realized in making them part of his "stock company." Thus the mythologized characters become "real," for they are the experiences of the audience, as Carradine was to discover when he was hissed, and Fonda was to realize when strangers called him Frank.

After Jesse James had been killed by Ford, Major Edwards of Sedalia, Missouri, wrote an editorial of ciceronian eloquence branding as eternally infamous the action of the state of Missouri in putting a price upon the outlaw's head and hiring "a band of cut-throats and highwaymen to murder him."

In his opening paragraph, Edwards remarked how vividly the young outlaw had seized upon the popular imagination:

> No one among all the hired cowards, hard on the hunt for blood-money, dared face this wonderful outlaw, one even against 20, until he had disarmed himself and turned his back to his assassin, the first and only time in a career which has passed from the realms of an almost fabulous romance into that of history.[23]

In arguing these impassioned sentiments in defense of Jesse James, the historical Major Edwards failed to reckon with the process whereby mere fact is transmitted into colorful legend. Because the materials of history are based on fact, history is obviously the truth; because the stuff of legend, on the other hand, is heavily fictive, it must therefore be false. But the truth is that Jesse James passed, not from "almost fabulous romance into that of history," but from history into fabulous romance. Cocteau once said that history is truth becoming falsehood, but myth is falsehood becoming truth.

There are two stories about Jesse James; one belongs to history, the other to myth. The passing years obscure the outlines of the former; but no mythic presence persists more vividly in American culture than the folk hero Jesse James. His granddaughter considered that "the only connection [King's film] had with fact was that there once was a man named James and he did ride a horse." Yet there is a higher truth than fidelity to fact--the understanding which prompted Aristotle's observation that poetry is superior to history, the former being timeless and universal, while the latter is limited in its connection to a particular time and place. Jesse James, incarnating as he does a figure that people want to accept as truthful, belongs to myth; in similar ways Stenka Rezin, Dick Turpin, and Robin Hood in their respective cultures become embodiments of populist attitudes. The fact that they are creations who loom outside history does not make them less true; the truth lies in the accuracy with which these figures represent widely held perceptions. As Picasso said, art is a lie that tells the truth.

The Western, in fiction, film, and in the fine arts, belongs to the genre of pastoral romance, of which _Tol'able David_ is also an example. Here again the country is of preeminent importance. As in the tradition of romance, characters are heightened and simplified, and issues of right and wrong are simplistically clarified. These conventions were served in the vividly rendered William Russell Westerns King directed from 1918 to 1919. Although King insisted that _The Winning of Barbara Worth_ was a story about the reclamation of the Imperial Valley and not a Western, that film focuses on the country as its subject; it features clear-cut villains--in this case Eastern land speculators, stalwart pioneers and defenders, and a blonde and blue-eyed heroine in accordance with convention. King's Western villains in _Jesse James_ are also "Eastern"; in this regard his view of the city is consistent with that offered by much early twentieth-century fiction and film.

Technicolor is ideally the medium for romance. Appropriately enough, King's next Western after _Barbara Worth_ was _Ramona_[24] (1935)--if one may call this romance of the Southwest a Western. King thought it the first (although it was actually the second) outdoor picture to use the process, and the color is vibrantly beautiful. (Of course the style of the period required highly saturated color; recently, color application has become much more controllable.) Again there are archetypes: a hero (an Indian brave), a beautiful heroine (a "half-breed"), a wicked stepmother, and an edenically beautiful countryside. The indigenous Mission architecture, the fruit-laden orchards of California, a sheepshearing, and a Spanish fiesta: those features uniquely emphasize a sense of region. Sam Fuller once observed in a Wim Wenders' film that although reality is in color, traditionally the convention for realism is black and white. Jesse James, then, is in color for a very good reason; whereas in King's most realistic Western, The Gunfighter (1950), the medium is monochrome.

At a time when Technicolor pictures were events because of the expense of the process, the decision to shoot Jesse James in color was fitting, not only because it was a dynamically appealing way of presenting the studio's biggest new star, but also because it was the most dramatically visual way of romanticizing the hero. Significantly, in the year of its release, Warners entrusted Curtiz with making The Adventures of Robin Hood (although production on that film had started a year earlier). There were two other big Technicolor pictures that year--the world's best known children's fable on film, The Wizard of Oz, and the epic romance Gone With the Wind.

Jesse James is thus not a film to deal with historical verisimilitude, nor could the details of killing, robbing, and terrorizing in themselves enlist sympathy. The legacy of legend--what people wanted to believe and what they selectively remembered--would be the stuff on which Johnson and King fashioned their dream of a rebel whose defiance defines the law, of an American who springs from the people and is more sinned against than sinning, of a "buckaroo" whose wide country offers him that mobility which is the essential character of freedom, of an individual who is propelled in crime by the very American ethos of success.

But not at first. Jesse, his brother Frank, his strong and clear-eyed mother, and their servant Pinky live on a pleasant farm overlooking a broad river in the green and rolling Ozark country. They know their neighbors and are respected for their integrity and determination; the James boys, after all, are "set in their ways." They live in a community with strong ties of loyalty--a loyalty which hardens into solidarity when members of this community find their welfare and livelihood threatened. The voice of the community, although a voice raised more often in indignation than in intelligence, belongs to the editor of the Liberty News-Gazette, Major Rufus Cobb. (Cobb, perhaps, may be seen as having met the limitations of the frontier in confronting "civilization" as a loner within the law, thus in a sense helping to justify with his passionate and angry editorials, the Jameses' "outlaw" behavior.)

The doctor who attends the ailing mother is also clearly their friend. The preacher in the pine-walled church who marries Jesse and Zee, tells Jesse that his presence is as "welcome as rain to the flower," a welcome his congregation unanimously echoes. Even two men in the saloon selected to apprehend Jesse are on his side and not the law's. And finally, those who represent the law--the Marshal Will Wright and the jailer--are more sympathetic to Jesse than to the outsiders who have come to apply their own vindictive version of justice. Those who side with Jesse are thus by local standards the most eminently respectable; they represent the literati, medicine, the law, the church, and the community of farmers and friends who gather in the Dixie Belle Saloon. The town is a prosperous, well-governed community with a much-respected U.S. Marshal. It is called, significantly, Liberty.

By contrast, the outsiders who come into Liberty and its environs seek to dispossess farmers of their land. Their purposes are extortion; their motives self-seeking; their instruments brute force and legal chicanery. In the brilliant opening scenes, King reveals three vignettes which become parables against injustice. Accompanied by two henchmen, Barshee, the agent for the railroad, confronts an illiterate farmer with an ultimatum--his land for a dollar an acre, else confiscation of his property. The man looks in confused helplessness. He makes an X and turns to his wife and two children standing forlornly outside their chink cabin: what are we going to do? In the second instance Barshee offers his hand in feigned friendship to a young boy; he then throws him to the ground and threatens violence in order to secure the terrified mother's signature. In the third, Barshee comes across a hard-working young man gathering firewood who introduces himself in a friendly fashion as James, Jesse James. The mother is shelling beans. The firmness of her refusal provokes the strangers into attempting to beat up the second son, Frank, so that they might intimidate the mother into signing. But this maneuver is checked by Jesse who has come by to investigate. Barshee is himself beaten, nicked in an exchange of pistol shots; as he sullenly wipes his lips, one can surmise that he is hatching a scheme to get even. Thus in these three scenes the oppressive power of the railroad is graphically demonstrated. The railroad is a force which destroys community, dispossesses owners of their rights, and threatens the bonds of family. Relentless and implacable, the railroad has become the mechanical embodiment of the industrial age, an iron monster demanding sacrifice as it cuts its inexorable path across meadow and farmland.

That night the James boys summon their neighbors to make what plans they can to resist the invasion of these alien forces. But the law and all the authority of wealth and power are aligned with the outsiders. Major Cobb speaks prudential counsel when he urges Frank and Jesse to hide out for a few days, for Barshee and his men, with the law on their side, will return with vindictiveness.

When they arrive, the James boys are not in evidence. Despite the Major's insistence that they have left, Barshee assumes they are hiding when he sees a light from the bedside of the invalided mother. Barshee and his men firebomb the house, and the mother dies as she is removed from the flames.

By this point it is clear that only in the most legalistic sense are Jesse and Frank outlaws. The violators of moral law are the unscrupulous and extortionate agents of the railroad. In the work of Henry King, as we have seen, the mother is the primal connection. To harm that bond, to injure the family, is to destroy something sacrosanct. Everyone is thus united in sentiment with the James boys; and when Jesse returns to shoot down Barshee in the Dixie Belle Saloon, it is at least understandable that Jesse undertakes the obligation to requite the evil which the suborned law cannot redress.

The law having acted in a morally criminal way, Major Cobb is impelled to write an editorial condemning lawyers and, presumably, the passing of a system where under a heroic code there was no need for lawyers. Moreover, the railroad will be shown to bring in outside authority to aid it in its aggrandizements and in its pursuit of Jesse; and this authority is itself corrupt. The judge from St. Louis is appointed by the governor who enjoys the confidence of the railroad. The Federal soldiers become agents of the law, and hence of the railroad, when they pursue Jesse. But they, too, are corrupt, allowing themselves to be deflected from their duty when they stop to pick up the shower of banknotes Jesse scatters from his saddlebags as he flees. Local justice in the person of Will Wright (a name obviously chosen carefully) is immobilized by McCoy. Thus the implication of the film is clear: local people are powerless to redress their problems, which are the result of vicious and impersonal forces oblivious to the common good; for cunning, fraud, extortion, and deception are the strategies of the St. Louis and Midland Railroad.

Jesse's story bears some instructive parallels with David Kinemon's in Tol'able David. Both are hardworking, exceptionally motivated, gifted with initiative, and devoted to their families--of whom the mother is the center. Both suffer grievous wrongs--David when his brother is paralyzed for life by the Hatburns, Jesse when his mother is killed by Barshee. Both set out, impelled by the nineteenth-century code of manly conduct, to avenge the terrible injury done their families.

David's antagonists, however depraved, brutal, and ignorant, are nevertheless human-scale. Greenstream could take care of the Hatburns were there a jail big enough to hold them. By virtue of his dedication, courage, perseverance, and tenacity (all individual virtues), David triumphs over the odds. His achievement is rewarded by the recognition of the community and the love of his mother and future wife. Before him through the valley of Greenstream unwinds the bright road of the future.

Jesse, however, is forced with his brother Frank to become an outcast of the community into which he was born. His antagonist is the railroad, and behind the railroad, nameless corporations and banks. The only human face he can confront representing these powers is the wizened and malicious McCoy. Jesse also has courage and tenacity and a quality which in the Renaissance nobleman would have been recognized as virtù. Told that he will be granted justice and a fair trial, he seeks an accommodation, if not a victory, with these forces that history inevitably will side with. But he is betrayed by McCoy's dishonorable reneging. After his escape, Jesse is permanently outlawed, and in his isolation becomes as bad as or worse than those who persecute him. Cut off from those who love him, Jesse cannot see himself, but Jesse is saved from corruption by the clear sense of Frank (whose name seems to suggest the shining candor Fonda brought to the part). And more than Frank, Jesse is saved by Zerelda who sees the wildness in Jesse's spirit. Zee recognizes that without her he is losing a spiritual equilibrium. Once she has joined him again with their son, the family is reconstituted, an event to which other events seem to move in King pictures.

Jesse wants nothing more than for God to bless his home. Just as David in the earlier picture is comforted on either side by his adoring mother and Esther, so Jesse is lovingly supported on either side by his son and wife. "I do love you so," she acknowledges to Jesse. Hence the dream of California and the West where the land lies bright because there Jesse, having left behind the wealth acquired by force, can begin life over. Jesse is convinced that it is time to leave when he hears a commotion caused by children playing outside the door. In the way that nature imitates art, the game the children are playing is Outlaw, and the outlaw in this episode is Jesse's son who in the persona of Jesse James is being killed. Being an outlaw, he realizes, is rough play. Only Bob Ford's shot will interfere with the decision to take the afternoon train. The sampler with its pious hope for God to bless the home crashes to the floor. Bob Ford thus takes his place with other traitors for whom Dante reserved the coldest place in hell.

But the ending in which Jesse is shot was controversial. Zanuck was reluctant to kill off his brightest male star; executives had long worked under the supposition that mortality meant bad business. Such thinking was responsible for the failure of 1934 in King's Marie Galante, for studio heads didn't want audiences to see Ketti Gallian die in her first picture. King wryly observed that the picture died instead when they tacked on an improbable ending. Johnson and King tried another scene, in which Zee says something to the effect that someone who is loved never dies.[25] But that didn't work, and Zanuck had the perception to see that it wasn't right. He concluded, screwing his courage to the sticking place, "We might as well commit suicide now as any other time," and the ending which Zanuck had originally suggested, the eulogy by the gravesite, was retained.[26]

The Jesse James which Johnson and King gave us was possessed of greatness. Like the classical tragic hero, Jesse also had his flaw; he let things get out of hand, so that what began as a personal act of honor ended in brigandage and plundering. In the words of Major Cobb who unveils the tombstone:

> There ain't no question about it. Jesse was an outlaw, a bandit, a criminal. Even those that loved him ain't got no answer for that.... I don't know why, but I don't think even America is ashamed of Jesse James. Maybe it was because he was bold and lawless like we, all of us, like to be sometimes. Maybe it's because we understand a little that he wasn't altogether to blame for what his times made him. Maybe it's because for five years he licked the tar out of five states. Or maybe it's because he was so good at what he was doing. I don't know. All I know is that he was one of dog-gonedest, gol-dangedest, dad-blamedest buckaroos that ever rode across these United States of America.

Despite the fact that Jesse lived by his guns, there was, as King presented him, a sweetness about him which seemed to belie the violence. He signals his presence to his confederates with a bird call; but more significantly, every time we see Jesse outdoors in the rolling Ozark country, there accompanies his presence the sound of birds singing, a phenomenon which suggests the pathetic fallacy, as if to say: this is the real Jesse who can inspire a harmony in nature not allowed of lesser mortals.

In terms of this picture, Jesse is finally defeated by a society that rewards treachery and grants amnesty for murder. The forces that destroy him for the audacity of his opposition are the mechanical gods that were to shape modern America. Ironically, Jesse plans his escape on the railroad whose coming he had so opposed. The fact that he has concerted all the power of his will against the machine which is also to be the agent of his deliverance is not entirely accidental. Jesse needs the railroad for him and his family to escape. This need makes evident its historical necessity; another manifestation of the force which must sweep all before the path of its "destiny"--Indians, agrarianism, and divisive animosities.

But there is another sense in which Jesse's opposition to the railroad in the 1880s could strike a sympathetic note in the 1930s. In 1938-39, as the country was recovering from a Depression perceived by many to have been created by ruthless individualism and the greed of large corporations, those forces were once again suspect. David Kinemon could drive the buggy whose power was that of pre-industrial America; but no one person could control the great machines that drew the continent together and which would annihilate the individual who set himself against them. The railroad joins the industrial East to the pastoral West, and the rails of commerce are laid upon Liberty. As big business in the post-Civil War years was the enemy of the little man, so in the 1930s that perception was widespread again. One commentator has suggested that the popularity of this film resulted from the fact that it offered an ideological focus for conflict, making that conflict conscious, so that, as Marx suggested, it might be fought out in an artistic form.[27] Throughout the Southwest, in Missouri, Arkansas, Texas and Louisiana, men, women, and children emerged from their hinterland fastness to see the incarnation of the legend which had passed down through generations.

It was King's custom to fly about the country to keep in touch with exhibitors to assure them of his personal interest in a picture. On one such trip King learned in New Orleans of the extraordinary reception accorded to Jesse James when a Mr. Landis, head of the studio's regional exchange, asked him when he was going to do The Return of Frank James. Landis explained to King, "Up in our our territory we have people that know Jesse James. They don't know who President Roosevelt is, but they know Jesse James. They've been following him all their lives." In one town, Landis went on, people had come to the theatre for the first time. "They didn't know you could turn the seats down, so they squatted on their knees to watch the picture."[28]

When King returned to Hollywood, he told Zanuck about Landis' question. Zanuck muttered something about exhibitors' selling the show they've got rather than one which hasn't been made. Shortly after, however, King met a writer in the corridor who told him he was working on a new project--The Return of Frank James.[29] That film, a more psychological Western, reunited five of the old cast under Fritz Lang's direction (1940). The popularity of the myth is attested by films that followed King's, among which are Jesse James (1948); Sam Fuller's fine I Shot Jesse James (1949); Nicholas Ray's inferior remake of King's picture, The True Story of Jesse James (1957); Philip Kaufman's more historically correct The Great Northfield Minnesota Raid (1972); and a conflation of popular mythology in the deplorable Jesse James Meets Frankenstein's Daughter (1966). Altogether, some 25 films have been based upon Jesse James, including an earlier one financed by the James family in the 1920s.

Jesse James, up to the time that it was made, was the most ambitious production ever undertaken in this country outside of Hollywood. The little town of Pineville was so isolated that only six months before its streets were unpaved, so removed that, according to Roy Pickard, talking pictures had not yet penetrated the district.[30] Pineville was incredulous that from all the obscure retreats of the world it should have been singled out as the site for a major motion picture. A special train arrived from Los Angeles at the adjoining town of Noel, unloading technicians, electricians, wardrobe masters and mistresses, make-up experts, stuntmen, cameramen, and a large cast, as well as two cars of Technicolor and photographic equipment and costumes.

When the filming began, it appeared that tourists converged in the area from all the 48 states. Some say that 6,000 automobiles clogged the roadways, others say that there were 16,000 or more spectators in daily attendance. In the midst of filming, Robert Webb explained to V. L. McFadden, a friend at the studio, how bizarre conditions had become. On August 25th, he wired to McFadden that 35,000 people passed through Noel on the weekend. On September 3rd, he noted that trains, busses, and planes were running special excursions, creating such crowds that King scheduled a fake location with a dummy company to deflect crowds from the real shooting at the James home.[31] On Labor Day, Webb reported on September 4th, excessive crowds had made shooting impossible. Certainly there were cars parked all the way from Noel to Pineville.

For 12 weeks there were gods and goddesses descending from the celluloid Olympus to explore the Crowder Farm, Big Sugar Creek, Crag O' Lea Cave, and Shadow Lake. They lived in Noel and worked in Pineville. Some native even suggested changing the name to Hollywoodville.[32] Webb remembered that when the crew arrived in Noel, it was a sleepy little place. By September 6th, he wrote McFadden that there were now 15 hotdog stands, 22 soft drink stands, 4 places selling cast pictures, 1 tattoo parlor, 2 fortune tellers, 5 popcorn stands, 3 balloon concessions, 7 ice cream vendors, 4 novelty vendors, 2 side shows, 1 "girl show" tent, and 3 "street shows" passing the hat. "So why not come down to Noel? Everyone else has."[33]

A strange new sense of reality seemed to transfigure McDonald County, completely refocussing attention as the film company became the central topic of conversation and the powerful source of an economic infusion. Fifteen constables and deputy sheriffs were employed by Twentieth-Century Fox to manage the crowds of sightseers, and 18 day- and night-watchmen guarded the equipment. Over 100 carpenters, 20 painters, and 60 laborers transformed Pineville into a Victorian country town. Eight inches of dirt were levelled over Pineville's newly paved streets. More than a 100 horses and rigs were hired locally. For the first time for many houses, indoor plumbing was installed so that the cast would not have to use outhouses.[34]

Nearly every major Midwestern newspaper sent reporters to Pineville to get a story; the Hollywood columnist Louella Parsons wanted an exclusive, and Jimmy Starr, a rival, one-upped her by coming out to the location. Life magazine sent the distinguished photographer Alfred Eisenstadt to do a special photographic essay. There were special pieces in well-known weeklies--Time, Newsweek, Liberty, and The Saturday Evening Post. The actors were the objects of such intensive scrutiny that from sunup to bedtime, their every move was followed by the Argus-eyed multitude. Henry Fonda complained to Nora Johnson, "We were never not being watched, while we ate, while we brushed our teeth. It was a new experience for me. You'd be sitting at tables with people lined up at the rope watching you, staring...."[35] Jane Darwell was even followed to an outhouse where she was interrupted by a boy who jerked open the door and snapped her picture with his box camera.[36]

Scenes were disrupted when spectators fainted from the heat, when bottle caps were noisily discharged from the sidelines, when the occasional native broke in to protest an injustice attributable to the film company. Yet for all these extraordinary strains, the area was so hospitable that some hosts had to be persuaded to accept rent, and few instances of inflated pricing were recorded. Meals at the Noel Cafe remained at fifty cents, and soft drinks sold for a nickle a bottle. The Shadow Lake Pavilion did booming business every night, and telephone operators could dance with the stars. "It's Shadow Lake tonight!" echoed around the film company with heavy humor as they realized how limited were their recreational opportunities. Every time Power entered the Pavilion, the phonograph operator put on "Alexander's Ragtime Band," Nancy Kelly danced with dozens of local swains, and Henry Hull went to bed every evening thoroughly soused.[37]

Further details about how the town disgrace, Lump Ward, cursed the movie company, about how Mrs. Crowder's prize guinea hens kept interrupting the shooting despite the fact that they were repeatedly sold to the butcher, about how Power's beard scratched Nancy Kelly's face, about how second unit director Otto Brower contracted poison ivy, about how three to four hundred locals were employed as extras, about what Fonda said to the little girl who didn't take his eyes from him while he ate breakfast--these and other bits of minutiae about the effects of the movie company on McDonald County have been carefully chronicled by Larry Bradley and Don Walker.[38] We learn that Tiny Stroud and Dabbs Greer went out to Hollywood; that the antique handpress used in the News-Gazette office was furnished by the Pineville newspaper; that Nancy Kelly bought a pair of overalls as soon as she arrived in Pineville; that Henry Fonda learned to spit tobacco; that Randolph Scott liked to go squirrel hunting; that Donald Meek when introduced to the Arkansas Attorney General confessed to cheating at solitaire.

There were three regrettable incidents: a visiting five-year-old girl was run over by an automobile and killed. And another accident could have been serious. In one of the most beautiful sequences of the film, Jesse's bold leap aboard the speeding train (doubled by stuntman Jim Williams), the silhouette of the outlaw is seen crawling above the cars against the twilight sky, while below the passengers are illuminated by the oil lamps within. George Barnes never photographed anything more beautiful; but the scene, obviously very tricky, had to be photographed from an accompanying vehicle running parallel to the train. One of King's assistants misinterpreted his signal, and King fell to the ground, suffering a concussion which later laid him out for a few days.[39] A third problem arose from the death of a horse. Otto Brower, the second unit director who was later to bring King back spectacular footage for Stanley and Livingston, filmed the leap of the horses from the bluff to the Lake of the Ozarks. One horse drowned, and needlessly, King explained, for a horse will swim if its head is kept above water. The rider failed to hold his horse's head high enough until he touched ground.

Pineville was never the same after the film company's three-month stay. Those memories which are still vivid are renewed every year. Just as Highland County in Virginia brings out an old print of Tol'able David to show each spring at its Maple Sugar Festival, so McDonald County in Missouri celebrates Jesse James Day by showing a faded and mutilated print of this handsome and stirring picture. The myth of the movie has become Pineville's living legend, demonstrating that Aristotle was right after all in asserting the superiority of poetry over history.

As beautiful, superbly paced, and winningly American as Jesse James is, it is not without imperfections which become apparent on repeated viewing. Why did Louis Silvers use the same "Westward Ho" theme and orchestration he had used the previous year in In Old Chicago? Were the resources of Twentieth-Century Fox, future home of the big musical, so limited? And isn't the preacher's reference to making an honest living before he took to preaching too easy a laugh? Tedious to the point of impatience is Cobb's running response to the people he disagrees with, that they--railroad presidents, lawyers, dentists, etc.--should be taken out and shot like "dawgs." But these are minor caveats in a picture of major successes.

In the words of Variety on January 10, 1939, Jesse James was "box-office smacko"--a sure "extended run attraction" with "all elements for top audience interest" including King's "superb" direction and "numerous sparkling performances." The film carried Power to the top, and for the first time someone surpassed Shirley Temple as the studio's number one attraction. Fonda found a laconic and wry screen persona which would serve him the remainder of his career. With Jesse James, King now had five pictures which, by the end of the decade, would rank, according to Motion Picture Almanac for 1940-41 as All-Time Best Sellers. These films were Stella Dallas, State Fair, In Old Chicago, Alexander's Ragtime Band, and Jesse James. Except for five from Chaplin (The Kid, The Gold Rush, City Lights, Modern Times, The Great Dictator) no other director at that time could boast such a record. Cukor, del Ruth, Dieterle, Goulding, D. W. Griffith, and Harold Lloyd had only two. Lloyd Bacon, Clarence Brown, Capra, Curtiz, Fleming, Ford, and Ruggles each had three winners. Only Demille and King Vidor had produced individually four all-time hits. Henry King was easily among the world's most successful directors. Still to come at the end of the decade would be the magnificently inspiring missionary story Stanley and Livingston (1939). There is a thread, as we have seen, which connects Tol'able David at the beginning of the 1920s with Jesse James at the end of the 30s. It now remains to see how King's next Western, The Gunfighter, poised between the 1940s and the 1950s, connects with the earlier body of work.

NOTES

1. Tom Stempel, Screenwriter: Nunnally Johnson (A. S. Barnes: San Diego, New York, 1980), p. 71.

2. Ibid., pp. 71-72.

3. Nora Johnson, Flashback: Nora Johnson on Nunnally Johnson (Doubleday: Garden City, 1979), p. 72.

4. Oral History. When Zanuck was trying to concoct a story around the Dionne quintuplets, he put King together with Johnson and Sonya Levien for a story conference that lasted ten days. Then King and Levien enclosed themselves in the Writers' Building until 2:00 a.m. the next day. That material, transcribed by a stenographer and typed by a secretary, then was given to Johnson who within a week turned it into a screenplay.

5. Of course Johnson had his successes with Ford: Prisoner of Shark Island (1936) and most notably The Grapes of Wrath (1940).

6. Oral History.

7. Ibid.

8. Larry Bradley, Jesse James: The Making of a Legend (Larren Publishers: Nevada, Mo., 1980), p. 29.

9. Oral History.

10. Bradley, pp. 30-31.

11. Oral History.

12. Ibid.

13. Bradley, p. 91. Bradley cites a Pinevillian, who, unfamiliar with editing techniques, expressed his amazement that "Jesse and Frank plunged over the cliff at Bagnall Dam, landed in the river just below Noel, and came out two miles south of town."

14. Don Walker, Fun and Games with Jesse James (McDonald County News-Gazette: Pineville, Mo., n.d.), p. 19.

15. Larry Bradley, Twentieth-Century Fox's Production of Jesse James (McDonald County Press: Noel, Mo., 1970), p. 11.

16. Roy Herbeck, Jr., "John Carradine Recalls Location Adventures of 1938's Jessie James," On Location (January/February 1980): 55. John Carradine remembers that the company had to send to Hollywood for riding horses because all the horses in Missouri at that time were trained for carriages and wagons.

17. Power and Fonda were paid $25,000. Scott was borrowed at $27,08.83, and Hull at $11,666.67. The rest of the cast were from the Twentieth-Century Fox stock company with salaries varying from Bromberg's $11,666 down to Darwell's $2,464.

18. Oral History.

19. Ibid.

20. Nora Johnson, p. 71.

21. Ibid., p. 72.

22. Fonda's next picture with King and Johnson was Chad Hanna in 1940; although pure Americana and vividly beautiful, somehow, somewhere, the picture lost its way and must be considered a failure.

23. Sedalia Democrat (April 1861) editorial found in the Jesse James production file, University of California at Los Angeles.

24. Previously filmed 1910, 1916, and 1928.

25. Stempel, p. 75.

26. Nora Johnson, p. 73. As Stempel points out (p. 71), this funeral oration was inspired by the editorial Edwards had written about Jesse.

27. Ed Lowery, Jesse James. Cinema Texas Program Notes, Department of Radio-Television-Film, University of Texas at Austin, 16 (1) (January 31, 1979).

28. Oral History. It is not too much to say that over the years King was able to augment Fox's revenues by millions of dollars through this kind of promotion. In one day he would fly to Oklahoma City, Memphis, and St. Louis; then on the following day to Indianapolis, Cincinnati, and Cleveland; and then on to Pittsburgh, Boston, and New York.

29. Fritz Lang's Western is similar to other Lang films in the same way that Jesse James reveals King's authorship of Tol'able David and The Gunfighter. "[Frank's] struggle against his fate [is] in the vein of the films from Lang's German period," surmises Robert Armour in Fritz Lang (Twayne Publishers: Boston, 1977), p. 121.

30. Roy Pickard, "The Tough Race," Films and Filming 42 (September 1971): 41.

31. Telegrams, Jesse James Production File.

32. Bradley, Jesse James: The Making of a Legend, p. 31.

33. Telegram, Jesse James Production File.

34. Walker, pp. 15-16.

35. Nora Johnson, p. 73.

36. Walker, p. 17.

37. See Fred Lawrence Guiles' account of the diversions of the stars in Tyrone Power: The Last Idol (Doubleday: Garden City, 1979). pp. 57-63.

38. See the works cited. Not reported were the liaisons arranged by the make-up man Ray Sebastian; these took place in Power's quarters in Mrs. Baughman's place near Noel. One girl after several such evenings became pregnant (Guiles, p. 61).

39. Henry King at Claremont, videotape, 1977. This accident was to prevent him from shooting the Northfield Raid sequence, which was directed by Irving Cummings in his stead.

The Gunfighter (1950): Jimmie Ringo (Gregory Peck) ponders the victim of his unwilling gunfight in a shoot-out in the Gem Saloon.

Chapter 7
The Gunfighter: End of the Trail

No fanfare of trumpets or roll of drums accompanies the familiar three-dimensional letters swept by searchlights which announce the studio created by Darryl F. Zanuck. Instead is heard a series of sharp, dramatic descending chords verging on the dissonant. A figure is riding across a bleak country of steep hillocks in contrasting shadow. This tall figure, darkly clad and on a dark horse, is riding from right to left, alerting the viewer that in the convention of screen language this rider is going westward. He does not suggest the familiar surrogate-knight of white horse and silver trappings.

From this opening it is clear that one will be watching a Western which does not subscribe to the usual conventions. The music modulates to a wistful air played softly on a mouth organ; and the introductory title rolls:

> In the Southwest of the 1880's the difference between death and glory was often but the fraction of a second. This was the speed that made champions of Wyatt Earp, Billy the Kid, and Wild Bill Hickock. But the fastest man with a gun who ever lived, by many contemporary accounts, was a long, lean Texan named Ringo.

Who was Ringo? The historical Ringo was named Johnny, not Jimmy; but the name Ringo and the few known facts of the real gunman made their contribution to the screen version. What is known of Ringo is clouded in an obscurity far more pervasive than that surrounding Jesse James. We do know that Ringo was a Texan and that he had a formidable reputation. In a seminal book which published accounts of the legendary gunfights of the West, *Triggernometry*, Eugene Cunningham takes respectful note of his presence, even though the material he devotes to him is scant. The book came to be a major resource consulted frequently by Johnson, King, and Peck; but one detail is not in the film: among the handful of photographs there is one of a heap of stones by a grove of trees--this is the grave of Johnny Ringo.

The famous Tombstone deputy William Milton Breakenridge, who survived into the third decade of this century, was the last person to see Ringo alive. At that time he was very drunk and headed for Haleyville. Breakenridge tried to persuade him to come with him instead and to stop the night at the Goodrich ranch, but to no avail. Breakenridge reports, "[Ringo] was found across the creek from the house of a family named Smith, near the mouth of

Morse Canon. His pistol with one exploded shell was beside him and there was a bullet in his head." Later, Buckskin Frank Leslie, a conspicuous character around Tombstone, argued that he had killed John Ringo, a claim thought by many to be doubtful.[1]

By the time of his death, it may be inferred, Ringo had become a mythic presence. Breakenridge was once asked by Cunningham whom he considered "the outstanding expert, both mechanically and temperamentally" of all the gunfighters he had ever encountered. Breakenridge replied instantly, "Johnny Ringo." "Ringo," he went on, "would have made me look like an amateur." Others shared his respect: "Johnny Ringo was one gunfighter none of the Earps wanted any part of."[2]

Partly from these materials, André de Toth--the man credited with contributing the story of The Gunfighter--found the lineaments of the character which Gregory Peck would ultimately portray. De Toth appropriated these characteristics: he is formidable, having no equal in gunplay, and having the temperament to be instantly prepared to take life without qualm if necessity demanded it. Peck had read that the gunman would have superiority over his opponent if he could decide beforehand that he would kill him[3]--and this characteristic is fully in accord with what is known of Ringo. Secondly, the filmic protagonist is also a drinker: he likes to drink in company but he also likes to drink alone, and he orders a bottle of rye at the table while he awaits his steak and pot of coffee. Finally, the real Ringo may have met his death from a man who wished to augment his own reputation at the expense of another man's life; whether Buckskin Frank Leslie did or did not take Ringo's life is not quite as important as the fact that he claimed that he did.

The genesis of The Gunfighter, however, is rooted as much in an American masculine ethos as it is in the mystique of the Western gunfighter and the tradition of glorifying the American badman. André de Toth is a dashing Hollywood figure involved since the early 30s in the direction and occasional writing of films. Among his close friends de Toth numbered Joe Louis, Errol Flynn and Humphrey Bogart.[4] At that time in Hollywood, the high life pursued by celebrities and those who wished to bask in their presence centered around nightclubs. De Toth noticed a curious thing: every time he accompanied Flynn to such places inevitably someone would challenge him, someone who wanted to demonstrate his prowess for his date. Bogart, he said, was especially vulnerable because "Bogie couldn't fight his way out of a paper bag." De Toth observed the same phenomenon when he went out to public places with the world's three-time Heavyweight Champion. Perhaps as part of the provocation he would hear some muttered remark to the effect that "you don't look so tough to me." De Toth realized that after a while his friends quit going out to public places because of the risk of such competitive challenges. The more he reflected on the currency of this phenomenon, the more he realized that here was the heart of a screenplay.

De Toth took the idea to a friend who was also a scriptwriter, William Bowers, at the time under exclusive contract at Universal. They were both working on the script of Pitfall (which was to become a tight little melodrama for Dick Powell and which de Toth was to direct); but since Bowers was prohibited from working elsewhere, de Toth, with Bowers' assent, carried the credit for Pitfall (1948). At the conclusion of that project, de Toth and Bowers began collaborating on the idea which resulted in The Gunfighter. According to Bowers, de Toth contributed the idea and Bowers did most of the work. William Sellers was a helpful presence who would not allow Bowers to put the script aside. In exchange for his encouragement, Sellers received equal credit with Bowers, but not equal remuneration.[5]

The screenplay would be written with ideas about the old West derived from original sources, some of them daguerrotypes and some of them from Triggernometry. The "hero" would be a man upon whom the countless incarnations of Wild Bill Hickock, Wyatt Earp and other gunmen had been patterned. Like Joe Louis, he would be at the top of his line of work; and like Louis he would discover that the champ is constantly in the presence of challengers. They had an actor specifically in mind for the role, an actor, who, like the hero, was now on the other side of the climacteric. His name was Gary Cooper.[6]

At the completion of the script, de Toth took the screenplay to Columbia. Columbia's chief executive, Harry Cohn, was interested enough to let John Wayne read it; de Toth reports that Wayne wanted the role so much that he put down a $5,000 option on the script. Cohn, however, was not interested and did not pursue the matter.[7]

Then the script was passed to Zanuck. Zanuck was looking for a prestige Western on the order of Stagecoach (1939), and a picture that would have a little more box-office appeal than that studio's critically acclaimed The Ox-Bow Incident (William Wellman, 1943), and John Ford's My Darling Clementine (1946). André de Toth argued that here was a script which would make an exceptional Western, especially if he could direct it and make it in such a way that it would have a different look. De Toth's vivid sense of color would later be manifest in the three-dimensional tour de force House of Wax (1953); but for Gunfighter he envisioned a Technicolor picture so drained of color that the effect would be sepia with sombre coloristic touches. Zanuck liked the script but he could not see any reason for using an expensive color process whose ultimate purpose was to provide so little coloristic variation. After all, the studio had just completed a decade of palpitatingly colorful musicals, films of such intensity that today their color has to be seen to be believed. Moreover, Zanuck didn't like the idea of going outside the studio to secure Cooper. Twentieth-Century Fox had a perfectly good male star who also projected strength and integrity. Why not cast Peck instead?

De Toth demurred. He didn't think Peck would do: he was too intellectual an actor, too contemplative a type. Audiences would remember him as the patient of Spellbound (1945) or the young priest of The Keys of the Kingdom that same year; he had also been the thoughtful journalist of Gentlemen's Agreement (1947), and most recently the tortured commander of King's engrossing Twelve O'Clock High (1949). The part, moreover, had been written for Cooper, de Toth argued. But Zanuck would not budge--neither on de Toth's idea for draining the color from the film, nor on his desire to cast Cooper. De Toth then sold the script, with Bowers' assent, to Zanuck and removed himself completely from the project. Zanuck turned the project over to Nunnally Johnson who agreed to act as producer and in several conferences with Bowers, Johnson assured him that the production would be faithful to the script.[8]

At some point before the final version (to which King had made his contribution), Peck was offered the leading role; he wanted especially to work with Henry King, whose direction in Twelve O'Clock High, so confident and knowledgeable, had stretched his abilities. He asked King if he had read the script. King had not but he knew of the project from Nunnally Johnson. Peck agreed that he would do the picture on one condition: if King directed it.[9]

At the time, however, King was planning a vacation. He had just completed two long and technically demanding works, Prince of Foxes (1949), his fourth picture to be shot in Italy, and Twelve O'Clock High, a film which must have been emotionally taxing despite King's Olympian calm. But when he read the script, after learning of Peck's interest, King agreed to make the picture and he plunged into pre-production work.

Zanuck and King did the casting, Zanuck suggesting either Colleen Gray or Helen Westcott for Peggy, Anthony Ross or Howard da Silva for the bartender, and someone like Claire Trevor for Molly. Zanuck thought Millard Mitchell perfect for the Marshall, who is Ringo's old friend and new adversary. Mitchell had performed in Twelve O'Clock High with admirable assurance. Six years earlier Mitchell had performed with Peck on Broadway in Irwin Shaw's Sons and Soldiers. Although the show played only six weeks, they both learned a great deal from Max Rheinhardt who was directing his last play in 1943. Additionally, they came to know someone else in the cast, Karl Malden, whose most important theatrical role would lie ahead--that of Blanche's suitor in A Streetcar Named Desire (1952). Malden was cast as Mac the saloonkeeper, a part to which he would bring in his portrayal of obsequious industry, a three-dimensional presence. The feminine lead would be played by a comparative unknown, Helen Westcott, whose stage experience was limited to nine years of playing the daughter in the Los Angeles production of the Victorian melodrama, The Drunkard. Her looks, however, strangely suggest Grace Kelly, later to be cast in Fred Zinnemann's High Noon (1952); certainly the two films have been often linked. Film buffs are always delighted to discover in the chorus of ladies, the presence of Mae Marsh, one of Griffith's great stars (The Birth of a Nation, Intolerance). Her career had declined after leaving her first director, despite King's having cast her successfully in Over the Hill (1931). This appearance would mark her 175th performance in films, and her third appearance in a Henry King picture (Deep Waters [1948], being her second). Jean Parker returned to the screen after an absence of several years in the role of Molly, described in the script as "a dilapidated young woman." Molly is the "singer," who has been left impoverished after the death of her gunfighter-husband. Although Parker had played some important roles in the 30s (Beth in Little Women [1933] and the lead in René Clair's delightful fantasy, The Ghost Goes West [1935]), she was terrified of being in front of the cameras again. King screened the Clair picture for her privately, complimenting her performance and assuring her that she could be equally good as Molly.[10] King was known for his ability to impart confidence; it was an ability that rescued Alice Faye as she was on the verge of leaving pictures; it had steadied two unknowns, Jennifer Jones and Jean Peters, in their first film roles. Finally, for the antagonist King cast Skip Homeier. Now a 19-year-old at UCLA, Homeier had been chillingly effective as the Nazi youth in the wartime drama, Tomorrow the World (1942).

For this picture King did not insist on extensive location work, for Cayenne, though vividly present in the picture, is a country of the mind. Nevertheless he would have preferred shooting in Texas. With the sensitive assistance of Lyle Wheeler, the art director who had worked for him on numerous pictures including his last three,. and with the vision of Arthur Miller, one of Hollywood's most versatile cameraman, King was able to achieve just the right bleak and moody feeling. Two days' location shooting were planned for Lone Pine, California--the desert water hole where Ringo disarms the pursuing brothers of Eddie, the "young squirt" of the Gem Saloon.[11]

Johnson was also eager for The Gunfighter to have a different look. He and King worked smoothly in planning the details, and although Johnson was the producer, King had his own way in one important and telling aspect of the protagonist's looks--his moustache. King felt that if he were to authenticate the sense of the late 1880s and early 90s, the look had to begin with the appearance of the three male figures. Peck was the first modern Western star to wear a drooping handlebar moustache; all the more significant because the dominant male look in 1950 was clean-shaven. (It was the Zeitgeist: the clean-shaven look is usually associated with the dominance of a militarist mentality: hence the look of Sparta, the late republic and imperial Rome, and Prussia.) In 1950 only such mature actors as William Powell and Ronald Colman still wore moustaches, and those were pencil-thin. Marlon Brando, Montgomery Clift, Robert Cummings, Glenn Ford, William Holden, Van Johnson, and Larry Parks were among the younger stars whose upper lips were never darkened. Characteristically the subjects of the daguerrotypes King had studied wore moustaches. He extended the look to Millard Mitchell, whose moustache was droopier if sparser. And as a young squirt eager to assert man's estate, Skip Homeier wore a skimpy growth on his blond face.

There was another reason King wanted Peck so adorned. King wanted to distinguish him in this role from his previous performance as General Savage in Twelve O'Clock High. Although it was Johnson who had given King Triggernometry to study, Johnson was quite dubious about the addition of the moustache. He knew what a sharp break with current fashion this feature would constitute. Zanuck was then in Europe, and in his stead at the front office was Spyros Skouras, a man as keenly sensitive as any to the mentality of the marketplace. Johnson knew Zanuck would object, and he decided not to inform Skouras. King instructed the make-up man, Ben Nye, to keep Peck's moustache at the exact same length for the entire shooting (the plot is set within an 18-hour period). Peck began to love the new addition to his appearence. After two weeks of shooting, Skouras looked at the rushes and screamed; the entire picture would have to be re-shot. King pointed out that re-shooting would add another $200,000 to $300,000 to production. Johnson let King have his way, but, uneasily, he knew that Zanuck would protest.

When Zanuck returned to the studio, King and Johnson ran the picture for him. Silence followed the showing. Zanuck groaned that he would give $50,000 (sometimes the figure in King's accounts is $40,000; sometimes $25,000) of his own money for Peck not to have that moustache. Zanuck was figuring the commercial consequences: "This man has a young following. That moustache, I'm afraid, is going to kill it." King pointed out that in the minds of movie-goers a change of clothes was not enough to mark Peck's transition from Air Force general to Western badman. "Oh, God bless you, Henry," Zanuck replied. "I'm not complaining about that at all. Frederic Remington couldn't have done it better, but I'm thinking of the box-office appeal."[12]

Others also assisted King in determining the authentic look of the picture. One of King's valued resources was Joseph Behm, who had also served as his prop man on Jesse James. Behm secured for King an 1870 slot machine for the saloon. Other support came from the costume department, for no aspect of the film received more carefully attention than the clothes, which were designed by Charles le Maire. King had Peck's clothes--which he called "a walking suit, only with a short tail"--copied from Western photographs of the period. Only someone who had lived through the 1890s would remember that boys wore hats, and thus all the schoolboys playing in front of the Palace Saloon are so attired. Jean Parker was fitted in a nineteenth-century corset, so tightly laced that it had to be loosened from time to time so she could breathe.[13] Impressively of the period is Karl Malden's brilliantined hair, slicked down in a curl over his forehead.

Thanks to Lyle Wheeler, Cayenne looks like a real place; the well-stocked general store is so darkly lit that one can almost smell the mustiness, and both saloons have ceilings. Saloons seem to be the outstanding architectural feature of Western towns. Here their spaciousness serves to enhance the solitariness of the central figure. The Gem, seen first at night, has brick walls shadowed in high relief; in Miller's photography they look clammy. The few customers of the Palace group themselves around the walls; and as the reputation of Ringo spreads, by late morning he is alone in the saloon, while outside may be heard the rising clamor of children's voices.

Cayenne sounds like a real place too: in the morning a cock is crowing and a dog is barking in the distance.[14] When the saloonkeeper's wife asks the Marshal if he'll have steak, the viewer half-consciously reflects that that's the way people often ate breakfast in the old West.

The patches of snow and the ladies marching down the boarded sidewalk with their shawls wrapt about them suggest the chill in the air; it is a significant seasonal touch because generally the Western locale is associated with heat, dust, and desert. The young children, in an interpolation entirely King's, throw handfuls of snow at the saloonkeeper. In this wintry setting, Mrs. Pennyfeather and her cohorts clothed in their dark garments and their black feathered hats suggest a chorus of blackbirds, congregating first in the store and then in the Marshal's office.

Miller had worked with King on the highly successful The Song of Bernadette (1943); in that picture his lighting, following King's instructions, had been most effective in creating certain numinous moments. "Good photographers are dramatists also," King once said. Miller's superb work in The Gunfighter, while relating to the brooding moodiness of The Ox-Bow Incident (a film in which Miller also photographed its night sequences in the studio), diverges from that photographer's best known work. There is fantasy and richness in his magnificently photographed The Blue Bird (1940); and equally an unusual warmth and sensitivity in How Green Was My Valley (1941). The look of The Gunfighter--no doubt supplied in part by such details as patches of snow, the stove in the saloon, unpainted buildings and muddy streets--is chilly and bleak, precisely the feelings which characterize the psychology of the picture.

* * *

"He don't look so tough to me"--this is the recurring comment which suggests that Ringo's real appearance is not in accord with his status as a myth. Everyone agrees that his reputation is extraordinary, so much so that Ringo's presence in a saloon induces hushed tones. What he carries with him is power, and in a raw country where quarrels were usually not settled with recourse to the instruments of civilization, sidearms were authority. In the old West, Cunningham observed in Triggernometry, quarrels were often fought to the death; and the gunfighter had to be psychologically prepared to risk death and mete it instantly.

The common element in the meagre historical records of Johnny Ringo, as well as in the fictive protagonist of The Gunfighter, is that by the end of their lives they have both attained mythic proportions. When Ringo pulls into the first town, he is greeted respectfully by an old-timer and the barman of the Gem; his reputation is acknowledged in the whispered recognition of drinkers and card players seated in the corners, and in the cocky challenge of Eddie, the young squirt who recognizes that despite the myth, he, too, is human--how many hands has he got? In Cayenne, Mac the saloonkeeper, with a mixture of surprise, delight, and a cunning born of utilitarian regard, reminds him excitedly of the old days, of Dodge City, the Mint Saloon, and Bucky Harris. "This place'll be famous, Jimmie. It'll be like a shrine. I'll probably have to put on two more bartenders!" Mac exclaims excitedly.

Three groups respond to Ringo's presence. The first group constitute the town loafers who pass on the news of Ringo's arrival to their acquaintances, the card players in the barbershop who value their health too much to leave their seats for the events that which will take place at the Palace--"looks like it might be a right interesting day." The second group is made up of the ladies' chorus who complain of the presence in their midst of a man who has killed 50 (the actual count being more like 15). They mix with equal emphasis their outbursts of outrage with expressions of domesticity: How long is a murderer to be entertained in Cayenne? How much are those potatoes?

The third group, also a chorus of sorts, is heard more than it is seen: the rising voices of children outside the saloon, their playful shouts becoming a descant to the dialogue within. The entire male population of the school has taken the day off, so excited are they by the presence of Jimmy Ringo. Outside they compare the presence of Wyatt Earp, another myth, as they peer under the swinging doors and through the windows. The child's vocation, as Wordsworth observed, is "endless imitation."[15] What these children are imitating in their play is once again the deadly game of their elders. Thus they are looped into the culture of the older generation. The background of children's voices is King's own substitution for a conventional musical background for cueing emotions. In addition to these groups, two individuals entertain a mortal interest in Ringo: they are Marlowe, whose motive is vengeance, and Hunt Bromley, described in the script as "the local tough boy not yet out of his teens. His ambition, obviously, is to be a pluperfect son-of-a-bitch and frighten people."

If Ringo's mythic presence is defined by the response of others to him, Bromley's character is suggested in the contempt of the children toward the aggressive teenager: "Jimmy Ringo wouldn't spit on Hunt Bromley." That character is also tellingly demonstrated in the barbershop when he barges ahead and takes the place of a man ready to seat himself in the chair.

Ringo then is the center of attention, his past converging upon him. He is at the end of the trail. As Nunnally Johnson said of him, "He's doomed.... He realizes he's just a clay pigeon." In some ways, Johnson reflected, "It's like Death of a Salesman."[16]

What does a gunfighter do when he realizes that his life has been a mistake? When he sickens of the bloodshed and longs for the peace and friendliness of family life? Molly, the dance-hall singer of the Palace, tells Peggy, the wife from whom Ringo is separated, that Ringo has changed, that now he's like her husband Bucky in the last year of his life, that the violence has fallen away. This change impels her to urge Peggy to see Ringo again. Bucky, "the second toughest" man Ringo had ever met, had also been a member of the same gang. And then there is a third gunfighter who has changed, also a member of the same gang, and who in the context of the picture represents for Ringo the road not taken: that is the Marshal, Ringo's friend Mark Strett, presumably of all Ringo's encounters the toughest man. Mark confides to Ringo, in an aside about which there is no other information, that after the killing, after he saw "the little girl," he rode as far away as he could. So he has come to Cayenne where now he keeps the peace of the community. He is conspicuous in his refusal to wear guns, a refusal which may indicate a way, perhaps, to break the karmic cycle.

Ringo is tough but he is also tired. He is 35 years old and he doesn't even have a good watch. Ringo knows that when Bucky Harris died--despite his eminence as a gunman--all he left Molly was a horse, a saddle, a pair of guns, and $15. There is a weariness accompanying Ringo's wariness--a wariness which must be unceasingly maintained in view of the ethical law that every action produces a reaction, every force a counterforce. Thus the gunfighter has not only to prepare for the constant challenge of competitive young squirts, of whom there seems to be one in every town; but he also has to deal with the survivors of those he has defeated (e.g., Eddie's three brothers); or what is the same, with those who, quite mistakenly, may think themselves injured (i.e., Marlowe). In King's fine Western (his last), The Bravados (1958), Peck takes just such a role--that of a man who mistakes those he kills for the killers of his wife, only to discover, after three men are dead, that his assumptions were altogether wrong. There are spiritual implications for those who live by the sword; the teaching is that they die by the sword as well. From the perspective of Eastern thought, the gunfighter must confront the effects of his causes, he must meet his karma. From a Christian point of view one reaps what one sows. One can be saved by grace through faith; but Ringo has not yet attained the desire to sacrifice or atone--he only wants to quit while he is ahead.

How much of his own religious sensibility King brought to the making of The Gunfighter is a moot point; it is probably something he would have been reluctant to talk about. Yet King's contribution of the presence of the minister, and the subsequent demonstration of the futility and psychic waste of vengeance clearly deepen the religious resonance of the picture. The greatness of the picture is that its spiritual implications bear universal ethical witness, for they are as consonant with Greek tragedy as they are with Buddhist or Christian teaching. Like Agamemnon, Ringo returns to the only place he can think of as home, for there is his family; he is slain when he thinks his fighting is over and he least expects death. Like Jesse James, he is killed just at the moment his hopes brighten and the prospect of a home with wife and child appear for the first time to be realistic. Like the tragedy Agamemnon, there is the sense of a net tightening as forces from the past converge. Like tragic drama, this film largely observes the unities of time, place, and action. But unlike the Greek tragic hero, Ringo is not larger than life--he is just a man tired of barroom poetics: there are no low-angle shots in this film to heroicize him. Ringo is inextricably a part of his environment, and thus the film is shot in deep focus.

A Sikkimese friend of the author remembers the coming of the first motion picture to the capital city, long a stronghold of a Vajrayana Buddhist tradition. The picture was a Western. He recalls that the audience sat amazed at the violence and fury of the actors, uncertain as to how they were expected to respond. They left the hall in puzzled silence. That reaction, in distinction to our own cultural mode, may be considered quintessentially "Eastern," if one may assume the Buddhist tradition to be the chief formative influence of Asia.

The term "Western" connotes more than the wide-open spaces of frontier lands. At one time it referred to strange seas and lands extending beyond the Pillars of Hercules. And it refers also to the European cultural tradition whose dynamism--aggressive, restless, seeking--has produced the United States of America (which are but a peninsula on the cultural continent of European thought); it has produced submarine and bathysphere to explore ocean depths, and planes and rockets to explore the firmament above; it has produced boxing champions and the MX missile. Europe and America are "Western."

The Western gunman (and his urban relation, the gangster) is the last incarnation of the European myths of individualism made permissible by Prometheus, Adam, Faustus, and Frankenstein; a myth which could flourish in the expansive, sunlit vistas of desert and prairie. The socio-biologist may be able to account better for the phenomenon than the cultural historian; but basically the gunman is a European fitted with a costume and persona for nineteenth-century America. The aggressive wielder of power, he is, in both senses of the word, peculiarly Western. From his point of view, value is the product of personal power; and the implicit statement in every challenge declares: If I can beat you, then I am better than you. It is the child's game of king of the hill or cock of the walk played with murderous weapons.

The gunfighter's aggressive assertiveness offers the American male, whose economic conditions painfully underlie his powerlessness, a potent image of identification, so that one can see in pool halls, in taverns near bus stations, on street corners in Boston or Richmond or Miami, men wearing Stetsons, smoking Marlboros, their psyches inhabited by images derived from film, television, Zane Grey and Louis L'Amour. But as King's film shows, the model of the gunfighter is ultimately tragic, containing within the cycle the success which is defined, inevitably, by defeat. Based as it is on the authority of physical force, the gunfighter can never transcend time, always the limit to the exercise of force which can only function in time (a point dramatized in Aeschylus' _Prometheus Bound_). Without moral foundation such victory is hollow. The Marshal, indicating the growing crowd outside the saloon, looks at Ringo and says, "That's your public, Jimmie." "Yeah," Ringo indifferently replies, "I'm a big man now."

Oscar Wilde once said that there are only two tragedies in life: one is not getting what one wants, the other is getting it. The poignance of the latter definition is evident when Mark looks at Ringo across the table: "That's the way you wanted it, wasn't it? Top gun in the West?" Ringo wearily recognizes that he's "got more people wondering when I'm gonna get killed than any man in the county."

What is happening in Cayenne is an indication of the change coming over the West. There is the schoolhouse. There is the church filled with members who are readier to attach themselves to the Rock of Ages than to the transient life of the range, the barroom, and the badlands. There is the staple of the small town and nexus of the masculine community which King was to glorify in Wait till the Sun Shines, Nellie (1952)--the barber shop. Then there is the chorus of ladies alternately exclaiming upon the outlaw and lovely onions, whose leader is the respectable Mrs. Pennyfeather. But most telling of the change is an episode which occurs midway in the picture: it is a half-hearted fight between two middle-aged men. Spectators standing about deplore the listlessness of their feckless engagement and remark on how much better fighting used to be in the old days. People are tired of fighting. The Marshal can separate them by dousing them with a pail of water; in the old days it took six.

As Robert Frost wrote in The Death of the Hired Man, "Home is the place where, when you have to go there,/They have to take you in." There is no place for the gunfighter to go, rejected as he has been by friends and family. "It's a fine life. Just trying to stay alive. Not really living--not enjoying anything--not getting anywhere.... Just trying to keep from getting killed."

He has tasted the bitter fruit of his success. As Robert Warshow has said, in what is probably the finest writing on the Western hero,

> Deeply troubled and obviously doomed, the gunfighter [i.e., that incarnation in King's picture so thoughtfully realized by Gregory Peck] is the Western hero still, perhaps all the more because his value must express itself entirely in his own being--in his presence, the way he holds his eyes--and in contradiction to the facts.... What "redeems" him is that he no longer believes in this drama and nevertheless will continue to play his role perfectly: the pattern is all.[17]

* * *

Although The Gunfighter was recognized as a film of unusual quality when it appeared,[18] its reputation gains luster with the passing years. One writer on Western films, Walter C. Clapham, argues that The Gunfighter is the paradigm by which all Westerns must be judged, the standard which some heavenly selection committee would put forward as the measure of all others.[19] The film clearly instituted the trend in "adult" Westerns. Just as Jesse James initiated a cycle of sympathetic outlaw protagonists, so The Gunfighter introduced so many weary gunfighters that the type has become a cliché.[20] Another critic, Allen Eyles, compares Zinnemann's High Noon (1952) to King's picture; he liked especially King's ability to find "truth in every situation," and the sense of passing time without the looming clock faces so present in the latter film.20 Now the King picture is usually regarded as the better film.

Looking back on his contribution in the making of the film, King recalled a few years ago, "You never know when you're making a classic. Babe Ruth didn't know he was going to hit a home run when he went to bat." What King said of Babe Ruth is certainly something that could be said of his own work with its occasional strike-outs. King continued:

> [Babe Ruth] fanned out as many times as almost anyone, but he hit more home runs than all of them. Every baseball player that goes to bat is up to hit a home run over the fence. Every director who's worth a tinker's dam is trying to use all his skills, all his faculties to put one over the fence.[21]

The Gunfighter is one of the memorable home runs in motion picture history.

NOTES

1. Eugene Cunningham, Triggernometry: A Gallery of Gunfighters (Caxton: Caldwell, Idaho, 1941 [1964]), p. 126.

2. Cunningham, p. 119.

3. Darr Smith, Los Angeles Daily News, June 27, 1980.

4. André de Toth. Interview with the author, November 10, 1983. Subsequent references to de Toth are taken from this interview.

5. William Bowers. Interview with the author, October 30, 1983.

6. Gregory Peck. Interview with the author, November 28, 1983. Gary Cooper had in fact been discovered by King in 1927 during the filming of The Winning of Barbara Worth. Among Cooper's famous roles was that of The Virginian (1929), in which he incarnated the archetype of the Western hero. Because of his success in The Gunfighter, Peck was asked to take the role of the protagonist in High Noon. He refused because he did not want to repeat himself.

7. William R. Meyer, The Making of the Great Westerns (Arlington House: New Rochelle, N.Y., 1979), p. 199. However, according to Jon Tuska ("Henry King," Close-up: The Hollywood Director [The Scarecrow Press: Metuchen, N.J. and London, 1978], pp. 58-59), Wayne turned down the role because of his strong dislike for Cohn who had humiliated Wayne when he was a contract player for Columbia in the 1930s.

8. Bowers, loc. cit. Although he was earnest about producing a serious picture, Johnson could laugh about the way

King and he were going to subvert the form. In an interview with Ezra Goodman (Los Angeles Daily News, October 24, 1949), he promised viewers that this Western would have no Monument Valley (Ford would complete nine Westerns in that location); there would be no chases; there would be no bearded rustic to act as sidekick; and there would be only two shots fired (there are in fact three). But because he did not want the audience to be completely bewildered, there would be "a fallen woman" to provide for continuity with the tradition. He reflected: "Always if you have four people in a carriage or a railway train in a Western, one of them is a fallen woman." Johnson's reference, of course, is to Ford's classic Stagecoach (1939), whose plot derives from Maupassant's Boule de Suif.

9. Max Freedland, Gregory Peck (William Morrow: New York, 1980), p. 103.

10. Meyer, p. 119.

11. Meyer, p. 201. In fact, the shooting was completed in one day. King shaved the extra time from the schedule by flying the cast and crew of 100 to Lone Pine in a DC-6 chartered by Joe Behm. The cast reported in costume, breakfasted on the plane, and dined on the flight back.

12. King was always aware as a director of his responsibility to others; to make a picture that would not sell would be an irresponsible act. He defended the decision as follows:

> I'm only interested in making pictures, and I want to make pictures that sell. I believe this picture will sell because it has interest. The thing that made us do it in the first place was the theme; as Nunnally said to me on time, here's a story about a man [who] has been bad and is trying to be good and nobody will let him! It's not a story of a juvenile. It's not a Tyrone Power vehicle. This is Jimmy Ringo. Go and look. (Oral History)

Despite this testament, the moustache, arguably, was commercially inadvisable. One writer (Meyer, p. 205) has noted that mail from 45 of Peck's fan clubs poured in to protest the growth on their idol's upper lip.

13. Meyer, p. 202.

14. There is no music track in The Gunfighter. As King asked rhetorically in an interview for the Oral History, "Where would it come from?"

15. William Wordsworth, "Ode on the Intimations of Immortality." The children's play is another strong link with Jesse James. In the earlier film, as disclosed in a script contained in the production file maintained by the University of California at Los Angeles, a child's voice is heard outside Jesse's house:

"Daddy, Daddy, I want to come in." Then is heard another child's voice: "He can't go in. He'll spoil the game." When Jesse goes out to investigate, the second child explains: "We didn't hurt him, Mr. Howard. We just killed him. That's part of the game."

16. Ezra Goodman, Los Angeles Daily News, October 24, 1949.

17. Robert Warshow, "Movie Chronicle: The Western," reprinted in Film Theory and Criticism, eds. Gerald Mast and Marshall Cohen (Oxford University Press: Oxford, New York, 1979), pp. 478-480.

18. On the whole, reviews for the film were appreciative and enthusiastic. For Bosley Crowther in the Times (July 7, 1950), the picture was "grown-up and distinguished"; Dorothy Manners in the Los Angeles Examiner found it a "new, almost documentary approach to an outdoor picture" (June 24, 1950); Edwin Schallert in the Los Angeles Times wrote that it "may definitely be catalogued as one of the year's best" (June 24, 1950). Life thought Peck "turned in one of the best roles of his career" and praised such authentic touches as "drab clothes and handlebar moustache."

The trade press, in an unusual departure from the custom of liking art less than the public, were even more responsive: "decidedly saleable merchandise in any situation," concluded Motion Picture Herald (April 29, 1950). The Hollywood Reporter (April 26, 1950) admired King's "measured direction" of this "arresting story set against a background of Pioneer America." Variety found that Henry King's direction "belts it over with the wallop of a prime Louis punch. There's never a sag or off moment... the scenes and characters have a vivid, earnest life, constantly hitting at the emotions" (April 26, 1950).

19. Walter C. Clapham, Western Movies: The Story of the West on the Screen (Octopus Books: London, 1974), p. 4.

20. See George Fenin and William K. Everson, The Western: From Silents to Cinerama (Bonanza Books: New York, 1962), on The Gunfighter. "By comparison with its imitators," Brian Garfield writes in Western Films: A Complete Guide (Rawson Associates: New York, 1982), "it remains the towering example" (p. 183).

21. Allen Eyles, "The Gunfighter," Films and Filming (June 1984): 28-29.

EPILOGUE

The road which unwinds to the limitless vistas of Tol'able David now comes to an end in The Gunfighter. The individual effort, as Stella realized, as Jesse discovered, collides with the implacable and amorphorus social forces whose powers are such as to sweep away opposition. There is something deterministic about the advance of the machine whose rails are laid upon the democratic vistas of agrarianism; something fateful in the operation of a society whose rules require that a woman sacrifice her daughter. To exercise the individual will as Jesse and Ringo discover is utlimately to act outside the law.

But to say that King's vision darkens as the century advances is only part of the truth. For him, the light of faith always seemed to shine, a faith that there was such a thing as love--his mother had surely shown him that, as had the two wives whose companionship he considered a fortunate blessing. There were such virtues as courage and truth; his own life was a witness to their reality. Thus, despite a dimming social vision, the virtues abide in the protagonist. And if a comedy is a happy ending, who is to say that King's life, as it now came to close, did not end happily as he opened his arms to what he thought was his mother, Martha Ellen, coming to welcome him? Of such moments of joyous reunion his pictures were emblematic.

THE END

Chapter 8
Henry King: A Chronology of his Life and Films

In 1688 Avery King emigrated from Ireland to settle in America. Among his descendants, John Howell King in 1861 joined the Confederate States Army ("H" Company, 54th Regiment). His son, Isaac Green King, married Martha Ellen Sumner and lived on a family farm two miles from Christiansburg in Montgomery County, Virginia. There were three children.

1883 Edward Reid King, eldest son, is born, June 10.

1886 Henry King is born, January 24.

1898 Henry King completes the last grade of a country middle school in Elliston, Virginia. Mr. Jim Graham, principal, congratulates Henry on a stirring recitation for an assembly; he tells King's mother that Henry has a gift with audiences.

Oscar Louis King, the last son, is born June 28.

Isaac King, the father, dies August 19.

1899-1903

Through the offices of Edward, Henry is employed in a variety of jobs working for the Norfolk and Western Railway in Roanoke, an important line which connects Virginia to the West. The steam engine represents the most exciting technology of the time.

Henry works first as a call boy in the trainmaster's office; he examines the pictures on the walls of the great engines of the world. He begins to study principles of combustion engineering, encouraged by his brother Edward whose interest is diesels. Edward and Henry go often to the theatre to see travelling companies and speculate about the actor's life, a highly unlikely dream for an industrious middle-class Virginia boy to pursue.

Ca. 1904

Henry lies about his age to secure employment as a locomotive fireman.

1905 Secures job on New York Central and supplements his earnings by lecturing on the Kincaid Stoker, a combustion device which Edward has demonstrated. Henry moves to Cincinnati.

1906 Now in Indianapolis, he enrolls in a dance class during leisure time under Professor Raynor (spelling uncertain). With the encouragement of his teacher, he decides to pursue his dream, and he joins the Empire Stock Company headed by Carlos Inskeep; the company is formed to tour smaller midwestern cities in repertory, vaudeville, and burlesque.

1907 Joins the Osmond Stock Company in Asheville, N.C. In the company he comes to know Anna Boyle Moore, a Shakespearean actress in decline, who tutors him in *Romeo and Juliet*, *As You Like It*, and perhaps other plays.

1908 Martha Ellen King marries Charles McDaniel.

King joins the Commonwealth Company for a three-week tour. He is then invited to tour with the Mason-Newcombe Company, a family troupe, for six months.

1909-1911

Joins Carlos Inskeep again in a new group called the Jolly American Tramp Show, whom he meets in Devil's Lake, N.D.; then he tours for three weeks in Myron Leffingwell's *The Minister's Daughter*. By this point King assumes leading man roles. Then King joins the Rowland and Clifford company in *The House of a Thousand Candles* (from the Meredith Nicholson novel) which tours California and closes in Chicago. King assists in directing the production. He meets Baker and Castle of New York who offer him a role in an aborted play, *Judas*. King takes the lead as Grenfall Lorry in the play *Graustark* (from the romance by G. B. McCutcheon). Baker comes to approve significant directorial changes initiated by King while the show tours for 40 weeks.

1912 Joins Paul Burns for summer touring. New York theatrical office of Al Woods secures King to tour in Robert Chambers' *The Common Law* during the fall season. The Henry W. Savage company attempts to engage King to tour in *Top of the Morning*; but when King meets

Wilbert Melville, producer of films in Pasadena, California, for the Lubin Western Studios Company, he accepts work in pictures instead.

1913 In a six-month period King acts in about 20 Westerns for Lubin in Pasadena. To pass time while waiting for his scenes, King begins writing scripts. King is asked to direct added scenes to completed pictures. In June King joins the Balboa Amusement Company of Long Beach whose pictures, produced by H. M. and G. D. Horkheimer, are released largely through Pathé.

1914 King is fully occupied turning out a three-reeler every week. In March 1914 he marries Gypsy Abbott.

1915 King develops idea for series of morality melodramas entitled *Who Pays?*; title for the first time appears at the end of picture. He is featured in this series with serial-queen Ruth Roland. King also scripts *Nemesis*, released as *The Brand of Man*. To produce violent effects in a fight scene he experiments with fragmentation of action in innovative editing. Other acting credits include *Should a Woman Forgive?* and *The Greater Love*. In addition to his weekly salary of $75, Balboa offers King an extra $25 for directing.

Martha Ellen King, Henry's mother, dies.

1916 Acts in a melodrama about mining filmed on location called *Pay Dirt*. In *The Climber* (four reels), he is a blond and blue-eyed Galahad of the streets whose chivalry admits him to society. Also stars in *The Stained Pearl* and in *The Crooked Road*. At a lunch counter he meets a three-year-old: Baby Marie Osborne becomes his leading lady in *Little Mary Sunshine*, the first film he entirely directs. She becomes immensely popular in the subsequent series whose titles that year are *Joy and the Dragon* and *Once Upon a Time*. He also directs the major part of a five-reeler, *The Main Spring* (direction attributed to Jack Conway).

1917 King continues acting and directing Baby Marie in *Twin Kiddies*, *Told at Twilight*, *Shadow and Sunshine*, and *Sunshine and Gold*. By her last film, her popularity (King remembered) is second only to Mary Pickford's. Directs Gail Kane, Spottiswoode Aitken, and Lew Cody in *Southern Pride* and *A Game of Wits*. Among his last acting credits are The Bride's Silence, Vengeance of the Dead, and The Devil's Bait.

In April King leaves Balboa.

In October the Balboa company collapses. Three Baby Marie films produced independently without him flop. Baby Marie is a has-been at six years of age.

King is hired by American Film Company ("Flying A"). Starting salary is now $350 weekly with a $50 weekly supplement to be added every six months. Begins association with scenarist Jules Furthman (a.k.a. "Stephen Fox" during World War I) directing the melodrama Souls in Pawn. Directs Mary Miles Minter in The Mate of the Sally Ann and substitutes for the leading man. Directs Sands of Sacrifice and Spectre of Suspicion.

1918 Directs the popular Mary Miles Minter in Beauty and the Rogue, her third five-reeler with King. Begins highly successful association with William Russell, personable leading man with Douglas Fairbanks aspirations, in series of thrillers, Westerns, and comedies: Hearts or Diamonds, Up Romance Road, The Locked Heart, Hobbs in a Hurry, When a Man Rides Alone, and All the World to Nothing. Also directs Cupid by Proxy.

1919 William Russell pictures all become five- and six-reelers: Where the West Begins, Brass Buttons, Some Liar, A Sporting Chance, and This Hero Stuff. The last Russell picture, Six Feet Four, creates in the opening sequences a country of the imagination uniquely distinctive; and there are interesting psychological resonances. Six Feet Four is billed as a "super-feature" and opens at the prestigious Strand. Henry King introduces Louis King to film as stuntman, actor, and ultimately as director. King leaves American. The company now decides to make only super-features.

King accepts contract offered by Thomas Ince, the studio head whose production methods changed Hollywood. Ince leaves, instructing King to take two minor actors, Doris May and Douglas MacLean, and "turn them into stars." Their picture, 23 1/2 Hours Leave, becomes one of the year's biggest hits; but King's option expires because the Ince studio manager resents King's practice of editing his film. Ince fires the manager, but by this time King has left for Robertson-Cole to make a series with the versatile young leading man, H. B. Warner. First film: A Fugitive from Matrimony.

1920 King's pictures with Warner for Robertson-Cole include Haunting Shadows (from The House of a Thousand Candles), Uncharted Channels, The White Dove, Dice of Destiny, and One Hour Before Dawn. King returns to the screen for the last time opposite Blanche Sweet as leading man in Help Wanted--Male (he shows an adventuress that love is better than riches).

1921 Also for Robertson-Cole he undertakes three pictures with the formidable Pauline Frederick: The Mistress of Shenstone (an English lady loves the man who killed her husband); Salvage (a tale of mother love); and The Sting of the Lash (an abused woman whips her wastrel husband). Just as King is to sign a long-term contract with Robertson-Cole, financial panic ends the negotiation. King contracts instead to make seven films for the newly-formed Inspiration Pictures under Charles Duell. His first film is the instant hit and classic pastoral romance, Tol'able David; it wins Photoplay's Gold Medal Award, then the equivalent in the industry of the Best Picture citation. King discovers Ernest Torrence who will become one of the screen's most menacing villains.

1922 Fate has cruelly decreed the survival of The Seventh Day (one of King's worst films--he admitted it was "a dog" despite the presence of some of the winning team who had made last year's hit) and the loss of two far better Barthelmess vehicles: Sonny, co-scripted with Frances Marion (a film specially praised by Heywood Broun), and The Bond Boy made the same year. Also lost is a remarkable drama filmed entirely at sea entitled Fury, starring Barthelmess and Tyrone Power, Sr.

King goes to Italy to film the first major American production abroad since the war, F. Marion Crawford's The White Sister. He discovers his leading man, Ronald Colman, in a Broadway play and introduces him to American films. Enroute to Italy, Archbishop (later Cardinal) Bonzano tells King that the film industry is as important as the university and the church in reaching humanity. This conversation is a turning point in King's awareness of the significance of pictures. King is advised by the papal master of ceremonies. Gish's taking the veil is one of the highlights of her acting career in a film which is a great critical success.

King's first son, Henry Edward King, is born.

1924 King returns to Italy for another Inspiration film starring Lillian and Dorothy Gish, George Eliot's Romola which is, however, more of a succès d'estime than a box-office hit. Duell tries to trade King's contract, against King's will, to MGM for two pictures. King refuses to be sold "like Uncle Tom"; Duell sues and loses.

1925 King grinds out for Paramount two routine assignments he despises; both Sackcloth and Scarlet and Any Woman are poorly received, despite Alice Terry's presence. Samuel Goldwyn, impressed by The White Sister and always scouting for quality, recruits King, promising half-interest in Stella Dallas from Olive Higgins Prouty's novel of sacrificial mother love. It becomes a box-office sensation, wins general critical plaudits, and provides Goldwyn as an independent producer with his first big hit. Goldwyn and King introduce Lois Moran to American films at 15. Jean Hersholt gains a new following and Belle Bennett is magnificent.

1926 King makes a disappointing comedy, now lost, for Goldwyn: Partners Again with Potash and Perlmutter and starring the popular comedy team George Sidney and Alexander Carr. Under trying conditions, King makes for Goldwyn the spectacular Western about the reclamation of the Imperial Valley, The Winning of Barbara Worth, from Harold Bell Wright's novel. King discovers a Montana cowboy named Gary Cooper and features him in a cast including Ronald Colman and Vilma Banky.

1927 King directs again Colman and Banky in a romantic circus drama, The Magic Flame (now lost), his last film for Goldwyn. King's second son, John, is born.

1928 The Woman Disputed with Norma Talmadge is King's first picture with sound effects. King shared directorial credit with Sam Taylor, who asked for equal billing, although (according to King) he directed only three scenes. On the other hand, some film historians say only three scenes are King's. (This writer, who was unable to see the picture, has no opinion.) What is certain is that King disliked this World War I Austrian high-society spy melodrama.

1929 She Goes To War is King's first part-talkie; it stars an uneven Inspiration cast: John Holland, a weak lead, Eleanor Boardman in drag as a doughboy, and Alma Rubens singing tearfully in the last stages of her heroin addiction. John Monk Saunders' prologue promises a picture to surpass all war pictures; but because of extensive cuts, the mutilated remnant is unintelligible. It looks expensive.

1930 King's first all-talkie, Hell Harbor, is notable for some sound innovation, some strong atmospherics made entirely on location in Florida, and an occasionally effective melodramatic turn (a man is killed when the lights go out in a Caribbean bar). This picture also exists in a severely truncated form. It introduces the first Cuban music heard in pictures, and the Habañera Sextette is a Latin delight. The film stars Lupe Velez and the feckless John Holland. King receives from Inspiration $175,000 in back pay and perfunctorily completes his contract with a picture which upon recollection he found embarrassing: The Eyes of the World, featuring Una Merkel (now lost).

Winfield Sheehan, Fox Studio head, approaches King to direct Will Rogers in Lightnin', a comedy about an amiable shiftless drunk played by Will Rogers opposite Louise Dresser. For the first time King scouts locations from the air, a practice he will follow for all location shooting. Joel McCrea is introduced in his first big part. This re-make of a 1925 John Ford picture based on an earlier play is successful and is the beginning of a warmly admiring friendship between Rogers and King. King is paid $50,000 for his direction.

Martha Ellen, King's only daughter, is born.

King becomes a QB (Quiet Birdman), a member of an organization formed by ex-World War I pilots to exchange information.

1931 Fox offers King a contract of $4000 per week, 52 weeks a year. His first assignment registers handsomely at the box office: Merely Mary Ann is an old-fashioned love story adapted from an earlier remake based on Israel Zangwill's play about an orphan slavey's devotion to a temperamental musician; it stars Fox's bankable lovebirds, Janet Gaynor and Charles Farrell. Far too sweet for modern tastes, but the "Kiss Me Goodnight" theme of the street musicians is charming.

King also makes one of his best pictures, the almost entirely forgotten Over the Hill, once Fox's biggest hit in 1920 when it starred Mary Carr. A solidly crafted tale of mother love, Over the Hill is admittedly old-fashioned, but it earns its sentiment and it is filled with memorable scenes. King innovates contrapuntal sound. The excellent cast includes Mae Marsh (whom King brought out of retirement for her first sound picture and her only starring role in the new medium); the well-known silent lead James Kirkwood; an engaging team, James Dunn and Sally Eilers; and Olin Howland, who plays a hypocrite of Dickensian proportions. Despite many sentimental opportunities, the picture stands on its own today and needs to be seen.

1932 Fox is in turmoil as Sheehan is rusticated during a period known as "The Rebellion." New executives rush bankable talent into pictures so quickly as to overexpose them. King is assigned a contrived murder mystery, The Woman in Room 13, creaking in its third remake, and does what he can. An impressive montage, glossy camerawork by John Seitz, and polished performances to little purpose from Elissa Landi, Ralph Bellamy, Neil Hamilton, Gilbert Roland, and Myrna Loy.

1933 Sheehan returns, and King scores a triumph in a delightful story of an Iowa family's journey to the State Fair. The parents seek prizes for pigs and pickles; the young look for love and experience. An excellent cast include Gaynor, Rogers, Dresser, Eilers, Lew Ayres, and Victor Jory. State Fair saves Fox from receivership, brings new life to Gaynor and Rogers, and becomes King's second "All-Time Best Seller," a term that indicates Motion Picture Almanac's designation for sensational box office returns. Only Charlie Chaplin was to equal King in the number of hits in this category.

One of his great pictures, State Fair stands in sharp contrast to his next assignment, an expensive but witless production, I Loved You Wednesday, starring Elissa Landi, Warner Baxter, and Victor Jory. William Cameron Menzies receives co-director credit. A confusing love story in which Landi must choose between a romantic roué and an uninteresting engineer.

1934 King takes on Paul Green's The House of Connelly without the miscegenation theme. Carolina, reputed to have some fine comic moments, is a "Southern," now lost, which includes Gaynor, Lionel Barrymore, Robert Young, Henrietta Crosman, and Shirley Temple at age six. Gaynor remembers being awed by Barrymore as an Old South patriarch. For his second picture that year King directs Ketti Gallian in a fruitless attempt to make her a star. The story, Marie Galante, is a Panama Canal spy melodrama starring Spencer Tracy. A studio-imposed happy ending killed the picture, according to King. The surviving print has the ending excised, so it is hard to tell. Some good locations and atmospherics. Helen Morgan sings a plaintive love song.

1935 One More Spring, from the Robert Nathan novel, is a romantic comedy set in the Depression which failed to click with audiences. The theme is that in poverty one finds joy by sharing, and so it is in the experience of a bankrupt antique dealer, a streetwalker, and an unemployed musician who huddle against winter and the world in a storage building in Central Park. Despite excellent touches, an exciting opening montage, and strong performances by Warner Baxter and the wistfully ethereal Gaynor, the film does not rank with Borzage's A Man's Castle (1933) and lacks the social vision of Vidor's Our Daily Bread (1934).

Way Down East would easily stand comparison with Griffith's 1920 version if King had not had to replace Gaynor with Rochelle Hudson, who is a dull and dispirited Anna Moore. King keenly regretted having to use the back lot and paraffin cakes for ice. Nonetheless, the story has a clear period sense (ca. 1885) to make it more credible, and is fresh and bright, and Henry Fonda, Martha Hamilton, and Russell Simpson are wonderful. When the harmonium plays "In the Gloaming" and the lamps are lit for supper, the scene has the quiet and intimate poetry which bears the signature of Henry King.

King helps to found the Sportsman's Pilot Association, Inc., the country's oldest private flying club.

Henry King directing Janet Gaynor in a scene in the lost "Southern" Carolina.

1936 King offers Zanuck his contract when he hears that the head of the newly-formed Twentieth-Century Fox is buying out Fox's old directors; King does not want to be anywhere he is not wanted. Zanuck is impressed and suggests for his next subject the Dionne quintuplets, who are now the world's most celebrated infants. King agrees, provided that he can tell a story strong enough to stand independently. The Country Doctor is a big hit and again revives the failing career of Jean Hersholt. One notable scene: a real priest administering the sacrament to a dying child in a diphtheria ward while the stricken mother watches helplessly through a window. One of Hollywood's most fruitful director/producer relationships begins with this picture, and King is shortly to become one of Zanuck's favorite directors.

Ramona, King's next assignment, is a third remake of Helen Hunt Jackson's Ramona, a tale of star-crossed Indian love. King expanded the concept of programmer and, in a pioneering outdoor use of Technicolor, makes a gorgeous and spectacular film starring Loretta Young, reviving Pauline Frederick, and introducing Don Ameche, whose previous experience was radio. King teaches him to use his hands; Ameche becomes a star.

Fox's biggest-budget picture this year is a polished historical fiction, Lloyds of London, about the founding and growth of the insurance company and its trials during the Napoleonic wars. This intelligent and very glossy picture introduces George Sanders who plays a cad superbly; but even more significant is King's discovery of the man who was to become Fox's biggest star--Tyrone Power, who is here cast opposite Madeleine Carroll. What looks like all of Hollywood's resident English community appears in this picture, which also stars Freddie Bartholomew.

1937 Seventh Heaven, a remake of Borzage's 1927 picture, uses exactly Borzage's set and set-ups for audiences who want to hear Chico and Diane talk. They are disappointed. Simone Simon pouts; James Stewart valiantly impersonates a Parisian and is charmingly improbable. Nonetheless, Roger Boussinot's Encyclopédie considers this remake "fort honorable," and one is never bored.

Zanuck commissions In Old Chicago as an answer to MGM's enormously successful San Francisco. The

On the set of In Old Chicago: King directs Don Ameche (Jack O'Leary), Tyrone Power (Dion O'Leary), and Alice Faye (Belle Fawcett). Cameraman is unidentified.

winning ingredients: handsome romantic leads, listenable music, and epic disaster. King dissuades Zanuck from casting Clark Gable in the part which consolidated Power's bid for stardom. King salvages Alice Faye from imminent failure as a result of previous directorial insensitivity and substitutes her for the role Harlow was to have played. Alice Brady wins an Academy Award as Mrs. O'Leary, Don Ameche starts his career as an amiable second lead, and the picture becomes an "All-Time Best Seller."

1938 Zanuck assigns King, now on a hot streak, a picture which is to become one of the great musicals, Alexander's Ragtime Band. Irving Berlin sketched the story which suggests his own career as well as the life of the bandleader who introduced new rhythms to the country, Paul Whiteman. (For his part Berlin thought this the best musical ever made with his songs). King brings together his winning triumvirate, Power, Faye, and Ameche, in a non-stop musical with 29 numbers and Ethel Merman. One song written especially for the picture, Now It Can Be Told, deftly and ironically advances the love interest. Notable for the presence of old-time vaudevillians from King's own youth, this film reflects the basic up-beat optimism about America which swing embodies, and is another "All-Time Best Seller."

1939 Jesse James is King's first Western for Fox and powerfully dramatizes in Nunnally Johnson's splendid screenplay the myth of America's favorite outlaw. A stunningly successful and beautiful evocation of the Midwest in the 1880s, the film, incredibly enough, is King's third "All-Time Best Seller" in a row. Backwoodsmen "who didn't know that Roosevelt was President" turn out to see this picture with Power, Nancy Kelly, and Randolph Scott; and, in indelible performances, Henry Fonda, Henry Hull, Jane Darwell, Donald Meek, and John Carradine. (Pineville, Missouri, has never recovered from its selection as the principal location.)

In Hollywood's year of finest vintage, Stanley and Livingstone is generally esteemed one of the 10 best. Phillip Dunne writes a very literate script which King partially revised, so that Stanley, instead of being an idealist, becomes a keen journalist in search of a story. The "Doctor-Livingstone-I-presume" sequence is movingly credible, and no one who sees this film will forget the Africans' jubilantly swinging "Onward Christian Soldiers," an inspired touch which was King's own. Three years of second-unit shooting in Africa lent authenticity to this remarkable inspirational story starring Tracy and Sir Cedric Hardwicke.

1940 Little Old New York is a falling-off after great success. A remake of a Marion Davies vehicle, it was not worth doing, but it could not have been done more professionally and carefully, despite Alice Faye's improbability as an Irish publican. Notable are the trial-run steamboat sequences at the end, which are supposed to represent Robert Fulton's experiments. Fulton is impersonated by Richard Greene; other actors are Anita Louise, Henry Stephenson, and Ben Carter.

Despite vibrantly beautiful color and a strong cast to present an itinerant circus in mid-nineteenth century America, Chad Hanna fails to come off, largely because the scenarist Nunnally Johnson can't decide whose story he is going to tell. Generally conceded a failure, even by King who admitted not knowing what to do with it. Cast includes Fonda, Dorothy Lamour, Darnell, Darwell, Guy Kibbee, and Carradine.

1941 A picture made to win sympathy for the British war effort before the United States linked hands with its ally, A Yank in the R.A.F. attractively combines Betty Grable and Tyrone Power; they are a striking duo who find themselves in London--he as a crass Yank who has much to learn, she as an entertainer who has a chance to sing a number. The flight sequences seem tedious largely because one is aware of mock-ups; apart from that, the picture is briskly paced with Reginald Gardiner and John Sutton. One notes with dismay a countryside in Kent with a eucalyptus grove and process plates of the Lake Country. The love scenes for this picture are budgeted at $235,000; the evacuation of Dunkirk at $100,000.

Remember the Day is one of King's most beautiful and tender love stories; a minor masterpiece, this picture revolves around the devotion of a fifth-grade student (Douglas Croft) for his teacher, effacingly played by Claudette Colbert. The set no less than the attitudes strikingly evoke mid-teens America. Delicate and lovely, the story is based on an episode in the life of Wendell Wilkie. Remember the Day needs to be revived and

Tyrone Power, as the boisterous Yank Tim Baker, teamed with with Fox's leading female star, Betty Grable (Carol Brown), in A Yank in the R.A.F. (1941).

needs to be seen! Also stars John Payne and features Anne Revere in a beautiful and uncharacteristic supporting role.

1942 Ben Hecht provides the script for an archetypal swashbuckler, The Black Swan starring Tyrone Power as a nice pirate, Maureen O'Hara as his reluctant bride, Laird Cregar as Sir Henry Morgan, and George Sanders as an outrageously funny red-wigged villain. Beautiful location photography by the man who is to become King's favorite cameraman, Leon Shamroy. Diverting but forgettable.

1943 The Song of Bernadette. Intellectuals are embarrassed to be moved by religious spectacle; but whatever one's proclivity, whether skeptical or devout, there is something to touch the viewer who stays the course for King's remarkable handling of the story of Bernadette Soubirous of Lourdes. What makes the film credible are the hard doubts of Charles Bickford and the flinty coldness of Gladys Cooper towards Bernadette's alleged vision. But King insisted that Jennifer Jones saw the Virgin where others screen-tested only looked. Jones' radiant simplicity, in a performance entirely directed by King, wins her the Best Actress Award in the Oscar sweepstakes. Glossy backlighting underlines the studio-nature of the project.

King leaves Fox for a year to help organize, at the behest of Washington, the Civil Air Patrol, an effort which helps appreciably to reduce the bi-coastal submarine menace. He is commissioned as Major.

1944 Wilson. Woodrow Wilson was Zanuck's hero of the century. Had his peace plans prevailed, the world would have been spared a second devastating war. King is given the assignment of translating Lamar Trotti's script into political epic. It is at five million dollars the most expensive American picture made up to this time; it is also unusually long, featuring a literal cast of thousands. It reminds Americans of Wilson's impressive domestic achievements in his first term and his patience in trying to keep the country out of the European war after his re-election in 1916. It makes intelligible the Fourteen Points and the need for some sort of supernational assembly of nation states. It also presents the problems of the Versailles Peace and the implacable opposition of Senator Lodge to American membership in

A moveland gala: Alexander Knox (holding gloves), who played the title role in Wilson, greets the then Vice President of the United States, Henry Wallace. Other members of the cast include Francis X. Bushman (to Knox's left), and (to Wallace's right) Geraldine Fitzgerald, Henry King, and Darryl F. Zanuck.

the League of Nations. There are 88 sets; and no expense is spared to make detailed reproductions of rooms in the White House, all photographed in beautiful color. Ultimately the Trotti-King-Alexander Knox portrayal of Wilson is perhaps unavoidably marmoreal, despite some attempt to suggest an idealism parlously on the verge of arrogance. King attempts to make the statue breathe by stressing the familial context: the President singing with his family around the piano, making gifts to his daughters, taking his wife to the Palace to see Eddie Foy. The chronological narrative is interrupted constantly by speeches more relevant in 1943 than 1986. When departing doughboys gather around a refreshment stand in Union Station for coffee, they are served by the President himself who gives them a fine speech but no coffee! This film had more power for those in the midst of the Second War and still more power for those who remembered the First. The names of House, McAdoo, Lodge, Daniels, and Edith Galt pressed more buttons then than now. A fumbled touch-down for Princeton at the beginning of the film prefigures the fumbled peace at the end of his political life; it also symbolizes how closely the film comes to victorious success. Wilson is a superbly crafted timepiece but it ticks only occasionally. Nonetheless, FDR had the film screened in the White House and "enjoyed it tremendously."

1945 King (of course) has not seen any Italian neo-realist film when he returns to Italy a quarter of a century after Romola to film John Hershey's A Bell for Adano, the story of the American occupation of an Italian town. The film has one magnificent moment: the return of prisoners who are greeted by their families in the town square--a homecoming which ranks with other such scenes in film history. From this picture, as from Huston's San Pietro, Americans learn that Italians view them as liberators. King was able to get across a certain gritty realism in handsome compositions, despite cinematographer LaShelle's penchant for glamorous shots. Gene Tierney's appearance as an Italian blonde is wildly improbable.

1946 Margie is a deft and affectionate entertainment, a delicate evocation of high school culture in the 1920s with rouged knees, raccoon coats, and cherry-picking Charleston dancers. Filmed on location in Nevada, the picture and the people have a real sense of place, and the dozen or so songs from the time are seamlessly integrated--Margie singing in the bathtub surrounded by irridescent bubbles, Margie singing in her bedroom as she prepares for bed, Margie waltzing with her father to "My Wonderful One"--the second time he has danced with her, the first when she was a baby. On the burning debate question in high school that year--should the United States get out of Nicaragua--Margie takes the affirmative. The film is also rather 1940s and reflects, as convention required, the hair styles of the time. Compare it with American Grafitti to observe (O tempora! O mores!) the revolution in generational sensibility. No one can fail to be charmed by the color, the music, the agreeable story and the delightful acting of Jeanne Crain, Glenn Langan, Conrad Janis, and Esther Dale.

1947 Captain from Castile is probably King's only film to go significantly over budget and whose costs exceeded revenues. It is a handsome spectacle which begins to sag midway after which it never regains momentum. The picture is notable for beautiful location photography in that most seignorially Spanish of cities, Morelia, Mexico--a locale where King made three pictures (prompting one critic to say that Morelia was King's Monument Valley). Jean Peters is introduced in her first role after winning a beauty contest in Cleveland and becomes a star; King, she gratefully remembers, made her feel secure. Tyrone Power's fifth picture for King also features Lee Strasburg, Caesar Romero, Alan Mowbray, and Antonio Moreno.

1948 Deep Waters, in its quiet observation of life in a New England lobster-fishing village, has its moments. A small picture with a fine cast (Peters, Dana Andrews, Anne Revere, and Dean Stockwell), it is flawed by a script that contrives an artificial opposition: Peters, a social worker, is opposed to Stockwell's learning to be a lobsterman. Because Andrews is her fiancé, he is forced to refuse the boy whom only he can help. Stockwell is excellent, and Mae Marsh gives a memorable performance as an anxious wife. A low-budgeted film, it paid for itself and brought back a small return. With Caesar Romero.

1949 Prince of Foxes is another Renaissance historical fiction, after a novel by Samuel Shellabarger. King returns to Italy a third time, now accompanied by his favorite cinematographer Leon Shamroy. The picture cries for color, but Shamroy is nonetheless able to evoke great richness in black and white. Orson Welles is superb as Cesare Borgia and Wanda Hendrix is badly miscast as a Renaissance duchess whom even Felix Aylmer cannot make believable. Power is more interesting than usual. The extras are Italian nobles who give their work for the restoration of the Ponte Vecchio. Everett Sloane could have stepped from the cinquecento.

Twelve O'Clock High. Although Wyler turned down a troubled story about the terrible pressures of men on bombing mission, Zanuck nonetheless feels that there are possibilities in this novel by Sy Bartlett and Beirne Lay, Jr. King, whose great avocation is flying, accepts the script and finds at Eglin Field in Alabama the location which effectively doubles for an English airfield. With Bartlett, King reworks the script to produce what Zanuck calls "the best script I've ever read." Twelve O'Clock becomes for aviation films what The Gunfighter is to become for Westerns: an engrossing psychological study rather than an action picture. The film traces the acute anxieties of the fliers who constantly gamble with death, and the awful responsibility of the commanding officer whose duty it is to keep up morale while simultaneously sending some of his men inevitably to their doom. For many years this film is required viewing at the U.S. Air Force Academy. Superb performances come from Gregory Peck, Hugh Marlowe, Gary Merrill, Dean Jagger and others.

1950 The Gunfighter marks a turning point in the evolution of the Western. Here the drama is psychological--only three shots are fired; and there are thoughtful philosophical implications in this study of a gunfighter who longs for peace but can't escape his violent past. Authentic period detail and Peck's striking performance make this picture memorable; Zanuck, who quarreled about Peck's handlebar moustache, thinks the picture "a Remington." A fine cast includes Millard Mitchell, Jean Parker, and Skip Homeier.

1951 David and Bathsheba marked Fox's response to DeMille's Samson and Delilah; unlike the earlier spectacle, this picture has substance, largely as a result of Phillip Dunne's fine script and King's serious consideration of the consequences of a godly ruler's adulterous passion.

Twelve O'Clock High (1949): Gregory Peck (left) as the troubled General Savage talking to Millard Mitchell in the role of General Pritchard.

"How shall I say the Twenty-third Psalm?" Peck asked. "Say it like you mean it," King replied. Susan Hayward wondered aloud why the film could not be called Bathsheba and David, and her star presence is one of the problems. With a small budget, King made a big-grosser.

I'd Climb the Highest Mountain was one of King's favorite pictures, but it is also his most self-conscious piece of Americana. It is literally, and qualitatively, Saturday Evening Post fiction brought to the screen in a formulaic blend of humor, piety and pathos. William Lundigan as the Georgia circuit rider is too weak, and Susan Hayward as his wife is too strong. They have a horse and buggy, ca. 1910, but a Chevrolet convertible would seem more appropriate. There are more magazine types than archetypes in this picture: there is an atheist whose heart is softened, a young rakehell in love with a good girl, a bigoted rich man who comes to see the light, a country doctor coping with an epidemic of "some new-fangled disease," a temptress from the city whose scheme for seduction is foiled by the pastor's wife and, finally, a Christmas in which old codgers discover what it means to give (the miracle of the dolls!). Tableau after tableau might serve as a Post cover; but Post covers, after all, are often quite charming in their old-oaken-bucket appeal. So why not enjoy the hayride to the picnic grounds, baseball in the meadow, watermelons at trestle tables, and a chorus singing with mountain inflection "In the Good Old Summer Time"? The film says as much about the 1950s as it does about turn-of-the-century America. The film is shot entirely on location in the mountains of North Georgia and just over the border in North Carolina.

1952 Wait till the Sun Shines, Nellie is a very strange picture. What promises to be a sprightly celebration of the American small town turns at midpoint into melodrama. The barbershop is a center of the community and provides the perspective to view the growth of the city. The barber (David Wayne) takes his bride to a town midway between Omaha and Chicago. The Nellie of the title (Jean Peters) longs for the bright lights of Chicago. When she realizes that her husband Ben has lied and will never take her there, she elopes on impulse with Ben's friend, a philanderer. But they never make it to Chicago because a train wreck ends both their lives. (Shades of Who Pays?!) Chicago brings no good, for Ben and Nellie's son grows up to be a racketeer with a Chicago crime boss and is killed in a gangland massacre (where? at Ben's barbershop!). But he leaves a daughter, also named Nellie, who grows up to marry the son of the town banker (where? only in America!). The subversion within the film is that the ties of family, religion, and law have been broken; and despite the paean to the small town and the rosy future the song celebrates, Ben's daughter and the banker's son end up leaving for Chicago. The small town is over. There may be more implications here than King wanted to ponder: the song says one thing, the film another. The barber is a small town sage who doesn't seem especially happy. But like King, he is a professional--he will shave anybody's face with a velvet touch. The changing tone of the movie is a risk King took to show what he didn't want to contemplate for long: the great change in America itself.

Screen history would surely have changed had King retained the studio's first choice for Nellie--Marilyn Monroe; King might have given her the confidence that would have changed her career.

King's wife, Gypsy, dies of heart failure.

O. Henry's Full House. In an uneven anthology King's contribution bests, in this order, those of Negulesco, Hathaway, Hawks, and Koster. Gift of the Magi is an exquisitely done turn-of-the-century Christmas story, the best known of the author's tales. Superb attention to period detail and irresistibly moving in its sincerity and intimacy. With Jeanne Crain and Farley Granger.

The Snows of Kilimanjaro. From Casey Robinson's script which includes abundant references to other Hemingway works besides "The Short Happy Life of Francis Macomber," King pares away many pages. He introduces for the first time flashbacks without dissolves. Except for the upbeat ending, which King justified by alleging that the final scenes sufficiently prepare for it, the film is a creditable transcription, as critics Gene Phillips and Lionel Godfrey conclude. In this version the hero gains insight from his wasted life and in turn is saved. The film launches Ava Gardner's career as an international star, an achievement for which King deserves great credit. The visual imagery works and Shamroy's photography and Herrmann's score are excellent.

1953 — King of the Khyber Rifles. King shows his professionalism (if not his best judgment) in accepting a dated melodrama which was old-fashioned when Ford made it in 1929 (The Black Watch). The Cinemascope screen, King's first attempt in the wide-screen medium, exposed a badly under-budgeted film in which 80 soldiers are supposed to be a British regiment in India. Terry Moore is preposterously unconvincing in her attempts at upper-class diction and is an unlikely Victorian lady. This film, about a half-caste who must prove his loyalty to the British raj by offering to turn against his adoptive brother, is a political embarrassment, made as it is five years after Indian independence. King wins the Directors Guild Award for the picture, although he considers it "pure hokum."

1955 — Power looks old and unhappy in Untamed, his tenth film for King, but Hayward never looked better. This film transposes The Covered Wagon (or one could say Cimarron) to South Africa and chronicles the settlement of the Orange Free State. Some good production values in an Irish hunt, a duel with whips, and a Zulu attack; and well-paced and better budgeted than its predecessor. Second-unit locations are recognizably and spaciously African. The film is easy to look at and moderately entertaining.

Love Is a Many Splendored Thing (from Han Suyin's novel) is a top contender for the Academy Awards this year and is a big box-office success. The love of an American war correspondent (William Holden) for a Eurasian doctor (Jennifer Jones) has a certain piquancy (even daring?) at this time; but the film now seems sentimentally romantic. The title song is one of the big hits of the decade. The opening (King's openings are always excellent) pulls the viewer from the air into the life of the city, and Hong Kong is perhaps the real star of the film. One strong moment: Jones practicing her calligraphy drops her jar of red ink at the moment when Holden is killed in battle. (The actors seem so in love that one would not know that off the set Miss Jones is feuding with Holden; at one point she angrily throws back at him a bouquet of white roses he has brought his temperamental costar as a peace offering.) The film is so carefully crafted that one does not know that the lovers on the hill are photographed thousands of miles apart from each other.

1956 Carousel. Frank Sinatra has been contracted to play Billy Bigelow, the circus barker. When Sinatra learns that the film will be shot in 55 mm, as well as Cinemascope, he walks out on the job, claiming that his contract specified one picture, not two. The cast and dancers are all assembled on Maine location and are waiting; the studio hurriedly replaces Sinatra with the likable Gordon MacRae who, however, lacks the feral charm and meanness Sinatra would impart. Shirley Jones is a replacement for Judy Garland who is too sick to work. Nonetheless the picture is handsome, the dancing spirited, and Lyle Wheeler's vision of heaven is arresting. Rodgers and Hammerstein are disappointed, and the picture does little more than break even.

The Directors Guild of America gives King the D. W. Griffith Award for Lifetime Achievement.

King appears with Tyrone Power in Sky Sentinels (directed by Robert Friend), a film on the work of the Civil Air Patrol and released by the United States Air Force.

1957 The Sun Also Rises in script form was approved by Hemingway in a conference with Zanuck and King. The sets are marvelous, and Morelia effectively doubles for Pamplona. There are two problems: the first is that Robert Evans' bullfighter is barely credible, a problem for which Zanuck is responsible (Bella Darvi told him that King's choice--a real bullfighter--looked like a waiter); the second is that one does not really care about this group of feckless and improvident wastrels, and Power is not strong enough to carry the picture. Errol Flynn gives a magnificent performance, his presence embodying a poignant lesson in mortality.

1958 The Bravados is a tale of unusual violence for Henry King. He revised the script so as to give significant spiritual implications to the obsessive vengefulness of a hunter (Gregory Peck) who implacably pursues four murderers whom he thinks guilty of his wife's death. This Western is also filmed near Morelia and sustains interest as long as Joan Collins is out of the picture, for her role is entirely a plot contrivance. King's regard for motherhood and the family are recurring themes in his pictures which are here obviously manifested.

On location in Maine: Henry King studies the script of Carousel (1956).

Henry King marries Ida King Davis and enjoys a contented home life in his final years.

1959 This Earth Is Mine is King's only film outside Fox since 1929. It is a handsome and lugubrious soap opera set in the Napa Valley. Gone is the attention to detail notable in Jesse James and The Gunfighter. The time is ca. 1929, but men wear crewcuts at a road house, and Rock Hudson wears a 1950s black knit tie and jacket. The flamboyantly theatrical Claude Rains plays a peasant patriarch as if he were an English lord. Although the patriarch has inveighed against the evils of selling grapes to the syndicate, Rock, the rebel, strikes a deal with Chicago, and everyone in the valley rejoices at the money Rock makes for them. Rock is the natural son of a woman who is paying with chronic invalidism for her adulterous liaison. The family live in palatial splendor with many servants, and are constantly arriving and departing in vintage cars; yet they are often warned that they are going broke. The Napa Valley has no Mexicans--only a Chinese manservant and tempestuous Italians. One earthy mama-mia type puts on hot water to deliver a child and refers to a baby as a bambino. Even the sense of the land seems forced; obligatory shots of grape pickers and young women trampling the harvest with all the realism of rag-finish postcards. A Dynasty episode stretched out to a yawning 125-minute melodrama, the whole effort is "product," an excess born of Cinemascope and too many violins. A Universal executive said King's work on the script was worth his salary, so valuable were his improvements. This is hard to believe, for the picture is one of King's worst.

Marie Osborne ("Baby Marie") is the wardrobe mistress on this production--an eerie parallel to the "morning glory" theme in Zoe Akins' play of that title.

Beloved Infidel (after Sheilah Graham's memoirs told to Gerold Frank) is curiously self-reflexive because there is a scene where a director (of King's age 20 years earlier) is seen directing an actress like Alice Faye who throws a jar of cold cream at someone like Tyrone Power. The scene comes straight from In Old Chicago; and in another scene Chicago burns. Had Peck been called by any name but Scott Fitzgerald, the film might have come off; but King seemed surprisingly insensitive to the fact that Peck resembles Scott Fitzgerald about as much as Fitzgerald resembles Abraham Lincoln. Both

Deborah Kerr (as Sheilah Graham) and Peck try gallantly with their impersonations. If the film were about people and not famous names (or, as Peck wanted it, if it were just about a writer), it would be an interesting but tortured love story. In life, Fitzgerald apparently was just not a scenarist: he couldn't do dialogue; but the script does not explain his failure, which Peck graphically and frighteningly portrays in a drunk scene which is a _tour de force_. One longs for more glimpses of life in the studios and in Hollywood.

1961 _Tender is the Night_ is a surprisingly good film which would have been even better had King had final cut. That prerogative is reserved to Selznick who seems to want to expose his wife as much as possible when less would be more. Cascades of memos are issued daily from Selznick to King who throws them in the wastebasket without looking at them. Jennifer Jones is harangued nightly by her husband whose advice sometimes is not the director's. In one production conference Selznick exclaims, "I don't get ulcers, I give them." Although some critics found Jones and Robards too old for their parts, Jones is an excellent Nicole and Robards is haunting as Dick Diver, a man who gives his personal and professional life to save his wife, who then becomes indifferent to him. A question: did it occur to King that Rosemary Hoyt (played unconvincingly by Jill St. John) was based on his Lois Moran, his own discovery? As the coldly mercenary Baby Warren, Joan Fontaine is splendid. One clever touch: King indicates the Divers' honeymoon sequence by showing a train entering a tunnel. The picture is sumptuously photographed by Shamroy and sensitively scored by Bernard Herrmann. Its great strength is Ivan Moffat's respectful and intelligent screenplay. Had King been able to edit the picture, he would have exited with an impressively successful film.

1962 King is converted to the Roman Catholic Church.

1976 King is invited to Telluride and several of his pictures are shown.

1979 King is given a retrospective by the British Film Institute.

1980 King is honored by retrospectives at The Museum of Modern Art and UCLA.

At 94 King becomes the oldest licensed pilot in the United States (with an unblemished record of perfect safety since 1915), and he continues to fly his plane until illness incapacitates him.

1981 He suffers a stroke in October.

1982 King dies at 2:36 p.m. on June 29 at the age of 96 at his home in the suburb of Toluca Lake in the San Fernando Valley. He is buried in Holy Cross Mausoleum in Los Angeles on July 2nd. Gregory Peck offers an eloquent eulogy.

ACKNOWLEDGEMENTS AND CREDITS

This book has been made possible by support from the Grants-in-Aid committee and the College of Humanities and Sciences of Virginia Commonwealth University. I owe a singular debt to David Shepard, Special Projects Officer of the Directors Guild of America, who made much of the research possible and who served as an invaluable guide, reader, and friend. I am also under obligation to Mr. Ted Perry who generously allowed me use of his interviews with Henry King for biographical background; to Professor Jack Ravage who made available important research on King's stage career; and to Mr. Larry Bradly whose materials on the filming of Jesse James in Pineville, Missouri, were most helpful, as well as his correspondence with a number of people who worked with King. Special thanks are due to Mrs. Henry King, whose kindness and cooperation have been greatly appreciated; to Ted Greene who offered me friendship and good counsel; to my colleagues Dorothy Scura, Robert Armour, Mark Booth, Maurice Duke, Richard Fine, and Bryant Mangum, who in their various ways rendered gracious assistance; and finally to the skillful typographic services of Gene Dunaway, who is responsible for the literal making of this book.

* * *

Some typesetting for the offset master of this book was provided as in-kind educational grant generously donated by Information Processing Consultants of Richmond (VA) Inc., using the NBI Independent Work Station.

* * *

Photograph Credits

Private Collection of Mrs. Henry King: Pages i, xvi, 9, 12, 22, 77, 91, 141, 148, 157; Museum of Modern Art, New York City: Pages 9, 114, 146, 152; Marc Wanamaker, Bison Archives: Page 36; The Henry King Collection, American Heritage Center Archives, University of Wyoming: Pages 54, 62, 71, 72, 92, 99, 143.

SELECTED BIBLIOGRAPHY

WRITTEN WORKS

Armour, Robert. *Fritz Lang* (Twayne Publishers: Boston, 1977).

Barthelmess, Richard. Scrapbooks on *Tol'able David*, 2 vol. (Motion Picture Academy of Arts and Sciences Library: Hollywood).

Bowers, Ronald. "*Stella Dallas*," *Magill's Survey of Cinema*.

Bradley, Larry. *Jessie James: The Making of a Legend* (Larren Publishers: Nevada, Mo., 1980).

Bradley, Larry. *Twentieth-Century Fox's Production of Jesse James* (McDonald County Press: Noel, Mo., 1970).

Brownlow, Kevin and John Kobal. *Hollywood: The Pioneers* (Alfred A. Knopf: New York, 1979).

Capra, Frank. *Frank Capra: The Name above the Title: An Autobiography* (MacMillan: New York, 1971).

Cherry, Richard. "Henry King: The Flying Director," *Action* (July/August 1969): 6-8.

Clapham, Walter C. *Western Movies: The Story of the West on the Screen* (Octopus Books: London, 1974).

Cunningham, Eugene. *Triggernometry: A Gallery of Gunfighters* (Caxton: Caldwell, Idaho, 1941 [1964]).

Denton, Clive. Henry King, *The Hollywood Professionals*, II (Tantivy Press: London, 1974).

Dunning, John. *Tune in Yesterday* (Prentice-Hall: Englewood Cliffs, 1976).

Eyles, Allen. "The Gunfighter," *Films and Filming* (June 1984): 28-29.

Fenin, George and William K. Everson. *The Western: From Silents to Cinerama* (Bonanza Books: New York, 1962).

Freedland, Max. *Gregory Peck* (William Morrow: New York, 1980).

Garfield, Brian. *Western Films: A Complete Guide* (Rawson Associates: New York, 1982).

Gish, Lillian with Ann Pinchot. *The Movies, Mr. Griffith, and Me* (Prentice-Hall: Englewood Cliffs, 1969).

Guiles, Fred Lawrence. *Tyrone Power: The Last Idol* (Doubleday: Garden City, 1979).

Herbeck, Roy Jr. "John Carradine Recalls Location Adventures of 1938's *Jesse James*," *On Location* (January/February 1980): 55.

Johnson, Nora. *Flashback: Nora Johnson on Nunnally Johnson* (Doubleday: Garden City, 1979).

Katz, Ephraim. The Film Encyclopedia (New York: Perigee Books, 1979).

Kirk, Cynthia. "Pioneers '73," Action, 7 (November/December 1973).

Lowery, Ed. Jesse James. Cinema Texas Program Notes, Department of Radio-Television-Film, University of Texas at Austin, 16 (1) (January 31, 1979).

Macdonald, Dwight. On Movies (Prentice Hall: Englewood Cliffs, 1969).

Meyer, William R. The Making of the Great Westerns (Arlington House: New Rochelle, N.Y., 1979).

Moseley, Leonard. Zanuck: The Rise and Fall of Hollywood's Last Tycoon (Little, Brown: Boston, 1984).

Moshier, Franklyn. The Films of Alice Faye (San Francisco, 1978).

O'Brien, P. J. Will Rogers (John C. Winston Co.: Philadelphia, 1935).

Pickard, Roy. "The Tough Race," Films and Filming, 42 (September 1971).

Phillips, Gene. Hemingway and Film (Frederick Ungar: New York, 1980).

Prouty, Higgins. Stella Dallas (Houghton-Mifflin: Boston, 1923).

Pudovkin, V. I. Film Technique and Film Acting, tr. and ed. Ivor Montague. Memorial edition. (Grove Press: New York, 1949; reprinted 1970).

Reich, Charles. The Greening of America (Random House: New York, 1970).

Rotha, Paul. The Film till Now (Vision: London, 1949).

Sarris, Andrew. The American Cinema: Directors and Directions, 1929-1968 (E. P. Dutton: New York, 1968).

Stempel, Tom. Screenwriter: The Life and Times of Nunnally Johnson (A. S. Barnes: San Diego, New York, 1980).

Stong, Phil. State Fair (The Century Co.: Philadelphia, 1932).

Thompson, David. A Biographical Dictionary of the Cinema (Secker and Warburg: London, 1975).

Tuska, Jon. "Henry King," Close-up: The Hollywood Director (The Scarecrow Press: Metuchen, N.J. and London, 1978).

Walker, Don. Fun and Games with Jesse James (McDonald County News-Gazette: Pineville, Mo., n.d.).

Warshow, Robert. "Movie Chronicle: The Western," reprinted in Film Theory and Criticism, eds. Gerald Mast and Marshall Cohen (Oxford University Press: Oxford, New York, 1979).

Winston, Miriam. The History and Development of Road Companies in Twentieth Century America, M.A. Thesis, Brooklyn College (June 1970).

ORAL HISTORY AND VIDEOTAPES

Shepard, David (interviewer). "Oral History of Henry King," conducted for the Directors Guild of America, November 1976 through February 1981. Maintained at the DGA Archives, Hollywood.

Perry, Ted. Oral transcripts of Henry King, 1976. Maintained at the DGA Archives, Hollywood.

"Henry King at Claremont," videotape, 1977. Maintained at the DGA Archives, Hollywood.

PERSONAL INTERVIEWS CONDUCTED BY THE AUTHOR*

Blankenship, Mrs. Mildred. July 17, 1984.
Bowers, William. October 30, 1983.
de Toth, André. November 10, 1983.
Gaynor, Janet. November 25, 1983.
King, Henry. August 14, 1981.
King, Mrs. Ida Davis. August through December 1983.
Hulette, Gladys. August 1981.
Marion, Frances. February 14, 1972.
Marshall, Mrs. H. B. October 18, 1980.
Moran, Lois. December 8, 1983.
Peck, Gregory. November 28, 1983.
Peters, Jean. November 25, 1983.
Rexrode, Mr. and Mrs. Kenton. November 25, 1980.
Simmons, Mrs. Luther. October 18, 1980.
Swecker, Mr. Scoop. October 18, 1980.
Wilfong, Miss Nona. October 18, 1980.

*Many subjects also made available primary resource materials (private letters, telegrams, clippings, etc.) in their possession.